What People Are Saying about

UNSTOPPABLE

"*Unstoppable* will touch your heart and [illegible] give more, take more chances and ultimately be more alive."

—Anthony Robbins, Author of Awaken the Giant Within *and* Unlimited Power

■ ■ ■

"*Unstoppable* will stimulate and challenge you to follow impossible dreams. They will never leave you where they found you."

—Dr. Robert H. Schuller, Senior and Founding Pastor of Crystal Cathedral Ministries

■ ■ ■

"The stories in this book are guaranteed to inspire you to believe more deeply in your dream and to motivate you to take the necessary action to make those dreams come true. I highly recommend this book!"

—Jack Canfield, Co-author, New York Times *#1 Best-selling Chicken Soup for the Soul series*

■ ■ ■

"There are three kinds of people: those who make things happen, those who watch things happen, and those who wonder what happened. Cynthia Kersey makes things happen and I have seen it firsthand. *Unstoppable* is a must-read for anyone who wants to make things happen in their own lives. It is guaranteed to be a runaway best-seller!"

—Kemmons Wilson, Founder, Holiday Inn

■ ■ ■

"*Unstoppable* is an inspirational book demonstrating by real-life examples how to break through the routine that sometimes makes it difficult to succeed in business and in life. I urge you to read this book written by a woman who is unstoppable.

—Ruth Stafford Peale, Chairman, Guideposts Inc.

■ UNSTOPPABLE ■

"Filled with inspiring stories, witty and moving anecdotes and practical tips on personal development, *Unstoppable* is a must to read and put into action."

—Thomas S. Monaghan, Founder and CEO, Domino's Pizza, Inc.

■ ■ ■

"*Unstoppable* is a must-read for anyone who wants to live a life where you grow until you go."

—Quincy Jones

■ ■ ■

"*Unstoppable* will show anyone how to live a life without limitations!"

—Justice Leah Sears, Supreme Court of Georgia

▪ UNSTOPPABLE® ▪

45 Powerful Stories
of Perseverance
and Triumph
from People
Just Like You

CYNTHIA KERSEY

Permissions

The author and publisher gratefully acknowledge the following artists and writers for their permission to reprint their work in this publication. Thanks also go to the individuals profiled throughout the book for allowing us to share their tremendous stories.

"Climb 'Til Your Dream Comes True," by Helen Steiner Rice, used with permission of The Helen Steiner Rice Foundation, Cincinnati, Ohio. Copyright © 1964 The Helen Steiner Rice Foundation—All Rights Reserved.

Pages 151 and 198 excerpted with permission from the American Academy of Achievement at www.achievement.org.

Page 19 cartoon © 1991, 1994 Henry Martin.

Page 40, 63, 76, 190, 237, 242, 263, 283, 288 cartoons © George Crenshaw.

Page 109 cartoon © 1996 by Randy Glasbergen.

Page 115, 168, 271 cartoons © Andrew Toos.

Page 122 cartoon by Robert Mankoff © 1987 from The New Yorker Magazine, Inc. All Rights Reserved.

Page 203 cartoon © 1994 H.L. Scwadron/Cartoonists & Writers Syndicate.

Page 278 PEANUTS reprinted by permission from United Feature Syndicate, Inc.

Published by
Sourcebooks, Inc.
P.O. Box 372
Naperville, Illinois 60566

Printed and bound in the United States of America.

5A 4A 3A 2A 1A

This book is dedicated to the unstoppable people who have made a commitment to pursuing their passion and unique calling with courage and determination. I admire your efforts and hope this book will provide encouragement and be a tool that will make your journey easier.

Acknowledgments

Unstoppable has taken more than two years to complete, including endless hours of research, interviews, writing, editing, and compiling information. It has been a true labor of love and the result of the combined efforts of many people. I especially wish to acknowledge the following:

To my husband, Dave, and son, Benjamin. Words cannot adequately express my appreciation for giving me the freedom to pursue my dream and for providing the emotional support to persevere through what seemed like a never-ending task. Your love and belief in me is my strength. Without your support and unselfishness, this book would not have been possible.

To the people who granted interviews and graciously agreed to participate in the book. Many of you have become special friends and all serve as a constant reminder of what is possible for anyone who is committed to being unstoppable. Thank you for sharing your life stories and for your outstanding examples of passion and commitment.

To my Mom & Dad who provided me with a lifelong example of love and support.

To my dear friends who believed in me and this book from the start. Thanks for your continual encouragement and insight.

To Denise Koepke, my dearest friend, who read and reread these stories countless times, provided invaluable feedback and endless support and enthusiasm for the project. Thanks for your love, support, and friendship.

To Jeffrey Reiss and Michael Gerber, for your enthusiastic support of my book and the commitment to bringing these compelling stories to television.

To Barbara Extract who provided valuable editing expertise and Sharon Goldinger who is an unstoppable copyeditor. To Karen Erbach, my research assistant, who enthusiastically embraced this project and helped identify numerous unstoppable individuals. To A.T. Birmingham-Young from the Giraffe Project who provided me with several potential stories including Laura-Beth Moore and Rocky Robinson who have both been commended for sticking their necks out for the common good. To Doreen Neser, the best librarian around, for providing assistance when I agonized over selecting the right title.

To Paul Orfalea, Founder of Kinko's Inc., for your friendship and willingness to make a call, write a letter or extend support to me on behalf of this project in numerous ways.

To Dominique Raccah, my publisher, and the entire team at Sourcebooks. Thanks for believing in my book and for your hard work and commitment to make it a success.

My deepest appreciation and thanks to the people who read the first or second drafts of the manuscript offering comments on how to improve the book. Your contribution was invaluable. Robin Anthony, Kathleen Breining, Susan Bregman, Kenny Binnnings, Rob Cain, Pam Cox, Randy Doyle, Dorothy Forbes, Millard Fuller, Terie Hall, Christopher Hegarty, Phyllis and Jim Hughett, Pam Jones, Denise Koepke, Barry Lou, Marianna Murane, Linda and Josiah Neff, Rick Normington, Meg O'Brien, Sherry Phelan, Dan Poynter, Anita Shaw, Blaise Simqu, Maureen Slater, Bob & Therese Wootton, Pam Ward, and to my niece and nephews, James David, Leslie and Stephen Hughett for enthusiastically listening to my stories.

And finally, to my dear friend, Millard Fuller. You are my role model and mentor and my life is forever changed as a result of knowing you. Your life's work is exemplary of true Christianity and I am eternally grateful for your support, encouragement, and friendship.

■ **"Some people come into our lives and quietly go; others stay for a while and leave footprints on our hearts and we are never the same."**

—Anonymous

Table of Contents

UNSTOPPABLE

Introduction

Your Heritage: The Unstoppable Human Spirit

How did a woman with no money, industry experience, or college degree create a $5 billion product line the industry giants missed?

How could a graduate student in a single week solve two mathematical problems that had puzzled leading mathematicians for decades?

How did a mediocre baseball player who couldn't hit worth a darn transform himself into a major league star?

What allowed a young man labeled "unemployable" by government agencies to become a top-producing salesperson and receive his employer's highest honor?

What drove a teenage boy to leave his African homeland and complete a perilous 3,000-mile, two-year journey on foot with absolutely no money or resources?

You will find the answers to these questions in the stories you are about to read. They are stories of the human spirit, of people who have overcome fear, doubt, and great adversity to achieve what the rest of the world saw only as "impossible."

Such "impossible" stories have been repeated throughout history. Where some of us have seen only limitations of the world or ourselves, others have gone on, with courage and imagination, exploring new worlds, achieving great dreams, ignoring warnings that "it" can't be done. The evidence of the unstoppable human spirit is everywhere. We have cured diseases, invented thousands of labor-saving machines, and forged roads across towering mountains. We have created global networks of communication and travel. We have touched the moon.

No obstacle has been too great for people who possess an unstoppable spirit.

Benefits of an Unstoppable Spirit

Progress is not the only benefit of the unstoppable spirit. People's dreams have come true, communities have united, and individuals have been inspired to try one more time.

From the greatest global achievement to the most personal accomplishment in our daily lives, the unstoppable spirit is the driving force for positive change and growth. This spirit is the force that breaks through countless personal barriers—barriers of self-doubt, negativity, and our own perceived limitations. It compels us to persist in striving toward our goals.

But how does one develop an unstoppable spirit? Is it only for those with superhuman abilities? Must one be born with a special gift? This book was born out of my own search for the answers to those questions. After reviewing and thoroughly researching the stories of hundreds of candidates for *Unstoppable*, I found the answer to be a resounding *No*. These individuals are not "superheroes." Most of them are just like you and me, experiencing their share of disappointments and frustrations. However, even in those moments, these people exhibit a few distinguishing characteristics that separate them from all others. These characteristics enable them to keep going when others would throw in the towel.

Seven Characteristics of Unstoppable People

Seven characteristics surfaced over and over. Unstoppable people:

1. Devote themselves to their true *purpose*
2. Follow their heart's *passion*
3. *Believe* in themselves and their ideas
4. *Prepare* for challenges
5. Ask for help and build a support *team*
6. Seek *creative* solutions
7. *Persevere*, no matter what the challenges

Fortunately, anyone who has the will to do so can develop these characteristics. To assist you in that process, this book devotes an entire chapter to each trait. The chapters are clearly illustrated with short profiles of people who have exhibited that characteristic. Most of the people in this book possess more than one of these attributes; however, I have placed each story in the chapter where it best demonstrates a specific characteristic.

In addition to the profiles of unstoppable individuals, each chapter includes a special feature called "In Their Own Words," an assortment of quotes, little-known facts, poems, and cartoons that support each chapter's theme. In various formats, you will meet dozens of individuals who transformed their dreams into reality. Each one has a different story to tell, and yet each experienced unstoppable results.

The backgrounds, goals, and challenges of each person represent a wide range of human experience. Some of the people in this book are famous; some you may have never heard of. Some were driven to found their own businesses, to excel in particular fields, or to make a difference in their communities. All were criticized or discouraged by people who branded their dreams "unrealistic."

Some of these individuals were highly educated; some had little or no education. All of them worked arduously, sometimes for many years, to reach their goal. Many of them had to transcend difficult childhoods of poverty, deprivation, and even abuse. All of them focused steadily on their hopes for the future, rather than dwelling on grievances of the past.

The one common link among all unstoppable people is adversity—they struggled, tripped and stumbled, and had setbacks and failures, but they pulled themselves up and kept on going. The dream demanded their all and they gave it. The challenges and hardships they faced seemed insurmountable and yet they surmounted them. With each trial, they emerged stronger, surer, and more deserving of the dream itself.

The stories of these unstoppable dreamers awaken in us our own potential to dream again, to act on those dreams, and see them through to the finish line. They illustrate that anyone—no matter how difficult their circumstances—can achieve their goals and overcome any obstacle, if only they will commit themselves to doing so. The qualities that assured their success are qualities that can be learned and developed by anyone with the will to do so.

That learning begins by reading their stories. They will inspire and instruct at the same time. The stories are short; none will take more than five minutes of your time. Yet within those five minutes are the keys to renewing your own abandoned dreams, of awakening new ones, and of translating your dreams into action. They are the keys to becoming UNSTOPPABLE.

Creating the Unstoppable You!

At the end of each chapter, you will find "Your Personal Action

Plan" with exercises and a step-by-step guide that will enable you to further develop each characteristic in your own life.

Maybe your goal is not to end world hunger, run a multibillion-dollar company, or make the cover of *Time*. Maybe your aspirations and desires focus on starting a new business, making a career change, or doing volunteer work in your community. Perhaps you've been wanting to run for a school board position, complete a 5K race, or pursue the passion for music that you abandoned for more practical pursuits. The size of the goal is not what constitutes an unstoppable spirit. It is personified in anyone who identifies a goal—something that *really* matters to that person—and refuses to give up that goal is achieved.

All you'll need for the journey is a notebook, a pen, and an open heart. The individuals you are about to meet will become your teachers, your mentors, your friends. They are role models, real and current, for what can be accomplished with a strong will and conviction. Wherever you are now, they have been there too. They faced the same challenges—and perhaps even greater ones—yet they continued to move forward. Their lives powerfully reinforce the idea that if we simply refuse to quit, we cannot fail. Every obstacle we encounter is a natural and necessary step on the road to achieving our dreams.

Learn from their experiences; take heart from their successes. Their examples will open new possibilities in your life and shift your focus from problems to solutions, from despair to an unshakable conviction that you can overcome and achieve anything.

Begin today and enjoy the journey of discovering the unstoppable YOU!

.unstoppable.

"The greatest natural resource in the world is not in the earth's waters or minerals, nor in the forests or grasslands. It is the spirit that resides in every unstoppable person. And the spirit of the individual benefits us all."

—Cynthia Kersey

Characteristic One

PURPOSE
Ignites the Spirit

The seven individuals you are about to meet in this chapter vividly demonstrate how purpose was the fuel that ignited their unstoppable spirits. Each individual focused on the pursuit of something motivated by his or her core being. When obstacles came their way, they used the power of purpose to propel them past the difficulties. Their goals were too important to allow anything to stop them.

On our journey together we will witness how purpose plays a significant role in achieving your heart's desire. If you have not yet clearly identified your purpose, you are not alone. Most people have not.

Located at the end of the chapter is "Your Personal Action Plan," a step-by-step guide that can assist you in identifying your purpose. Once you tap into its power, you too will become unstoppable!

■ **"Obstacles cannot crush me,**
Every obstacle yields to stern resolve,
He who is fixed to a star does not change his mind."

—Leonardo da Vinci

UNSTOPPABLE

She Pushed the Envelope of Compassion

One Mother's Mass Mailings from the Heart

Every week, Linda Bremner sends a thousand letters to children she doesn't even know. Some parents might not like their children getting letters from a stranger. But not these moms and dads. They write back to thank her—and so do the parents. Linda's letters give their kids hope, keep them alive a little longer, or just brighten their days when they see the postal carrier coming up the walk with the day's mail.

That's how it started—with the daily mail. In November 1980, Linda's eight-year-old son, Andy, was diagnosed with non-Hodgkin's lymphoma. After he returned home from his first hospital stay, he was welcomed with dozens of cards and letters from friends and relatives.

"No matter how bad he felt before the mailman arrived," Linda remembered, "he always felt better afterward."

Inevitably, however, the flood of cards and letters tapered off. So did Andy's cheerful spirit. Concerned, Linda mailed him a note she wrote herself and signed it "Your secret pal." Andy perked up. After that, Linda never let a day go by without putting another cheerful message in the mail for her little boy.

After sending Andy letters for nearly a month, Linda found him one day drawing a picture of two unicorns. It was for his "secret pal," he said. After putting Andy to bed that night, Linda picked up the drawing. At the bottom, he had written "P.S. Mom, I love you."

He had known all along who was sending him the letters! But that didn't matter—what mattered was that they made him happy and lifted his spirits. Andy's precious life ended less than four years later; he died on August 31, 1984.

"Although I had two other wonderful children," Linda remembered, "the grief and pain of losing Andy was unbearable. I felt my life was over because his was over." Sorting through her son's belongings, she found a shoebox in his closet. Inside the box was his address book listing all the friends he'd made at a "cancer camp" not long before he died. The address book gave Linda the idea that Andy would have liked her to be a "secret pal" to his sick friends the way she'd been to him.

She decided to send one card to each child in Andy's book. Before she'd gotten through the list, one twelve-year-old boy wrote to thank her. In his letter he told her, "I didn't think anyone knew I was alive." Those words made Linda realize someone else was hurting besides herself. She cried bitterly, not for herself or for Andy this time, but for the lonely, scared child who needed to know someone cared.

Just after responding to that boy's letter, she received a similar note from another child on Andy's list. That was it. She had found her calling, a purpose that gave passion and meaning to her life. She vowed then to write to any child who needed her until they stopped writing her back.

Her cards and letters were brief, positive, and always personalized. The children responded continually and their parents did too, each thanking her for renewing life in their child. Linda got friends and neighbors to help with her mission, and an organization of letter writers began to form. They named their new group Love Letters, Inc.

Together, Linda and her small band of volunteers worked tirelessly to help children beat the odds. Yet Love Letters soon discovered a myriad of challenges they were forced to overcome. The demand for their services was great and yet their resources were small. No mailing was complete without concern for where the money for postage or production work would come from. Working out of a temporary, donated space, the group survived from week to week on donations of stamps, money, and office supplies from the community and groups like the Rotary Club and Junior Chamber of Commerce.

Love Letters applied to more than forty corporations for grants and donations. Every application was turned down. Yet Love Letters never missed a mailing. The children meant too much to Linda and her thirty-five volunteers. Somehow people always came through—with a bake sale, a T-shirt sale, or just by reaching into their pockets.

Today, over ten years after Linda wrote her first letter to a child she'd never met, Love Letters, Inc., sends out more than 60,000 pieces of mail a year. The group's resources are still inadequate, but their resolve abounds. Thirty-five volunteers collectively contribute 400 hours for each weekly mailing. In addition to sending letters to 1,100 kids every week, it sends an additional 90 to 110 birthday gifts each month. For children going through a particularly difficult period, Love Letters makes sure something arrives in the mail every single day. Every year, Love Letters loses some 200 children who have gotten better or passed away. Sadly, Love Letters always has new names to add to its mailing list.

Linda personally puts in seventy to eighty hours a week to keep Love Letters going. When weariness threatens to overcome her, the telephone rings—it's another child or parent calling to say how important the program is.

"It rejuvenates me," she said, "because I have experienced firsthand the power of a love letter in healing the soul."

As much as she gives, Linda Bremner receives more in return: a reason for living, a vehicle for loving, a sense of purpose.

■ "I'm doing what I am doing for the rest of my life because it's so important. I've seen a child cry and I've seen a child smile. I like the smiles, and it's really important to me to know that I helped make one."

—Linda Bremner

.unstoppable.

"If I can stop one heart from breaking,
I shall not live in vain;
If I can ease one life the aching,
Or cool one pain,
Or help one fainting robin
Unto his nest again,
I shall not live in vain."

—Emily Dickinson
If I Can Stop One Heart from Breaking

UNSTOPPABLE

Mission on the March

A Barefoot Ulysses and His Incredible Journey

He possessed a five-day supply of food, a Bible and *The Pilgrim's Progress* (his two treasures), a small ax for protection, and a blanket. With these, Legson Kayira eagerly set out on the journey of his life. He was going to walk from his tribal village in Nyasaland, north across the wilderness of East Africa to Cairo, where he would board a ship to America to get a college education.

It was October 1958. Legson was sixteen or seventeen years old, his mother wasn't sure. His parents were illiterate and didn't know exactly where America was or how far. But they reluctantly gave their blessing to his journey.

To Legson, it was a journey derived from a dream—no matter how ill-conceived—that fueled his determination to get an education. He wanted to be like his hero, Abraham Lincoln, who had risen from poverty to become an American president, then fought tirelessly to help free the slaves. He wanted to be like Booker T. Washington, who had cast off the shackles of slavery to become a great American reformer and educator, giving hope and dignity to himself and to his race.

Like these great role models, Legson wanted to serve mankind, to make a difference in the world. To realize his goal, he needed a first-rate education. He knew the best place to get it was in America.

Forget that Legson didn't have a penny to his name or a way to pay for his ship fare.

Forget that he had no idea what college he would attend or if he would even be accepted.

Forget that Cairo was 3,000 miles away and in between were hundreds of tribes that spoke more than fifty different languages, none of which Legson knew.

Forget all that. Legson did. He had to. He put everything out of his mind except the dream of getting to the land where he could shape his own destiny.

He hadn't always been so determined. As a young boy, he sometimes used his poverty as an excuse for not doing his best at school or for not accomplishing something. *I am just a poor child,* he had told himself. *What can I do?*

Like many of his friends in the village, it was easy for Legson to believe that studying was a waste of time for a poor boy from the town of Karongo in Nyasaland. Then, in books provided by missionaries, he discovered Abraham Lincoln and Booker T. Washington. Their stories inspired him to envision more for his life, and he realized that an education was the first step. So he conceived the idea for his walk to Cairo.

After five full days of trekking across the rugged African terrain, Legson had covered only 25 miles. He was already out of food, his water was running out, and he had no money. To travel the distance of 2,975 additional miles seemed impossible. Yet to turn back was to give up, to resign himself to a life of poverty and ignorance.

I will not stop until I reach America, he promised himself. *Or until I die trying.* He continued on.

Sometimes he walked with strangers. Most of the time he walked alone. He entered each new village cautiously, not knowing whether the natives were hostile or friendly. Sometimes he found work and shelter. Many nights he slept under the stars. He foraged for wild fruits and berries and other edible plants. He became thin and weak.

A fever struck him and he fell gravely ill. Kind strangers treated him with herbal medicines and offered him a place to rest and convalesce. Weary and demoralized, Legson considered turning back. Perhaps it was better to go home, he reasoned, than to continue this seemingly foolish journey and risk his life.

Instead, Legson turned to his two books, reading the familiar words that renewed his faith in himself and in his goal. He continued on. On January 19, 1960, fifteen months after he began his perilous journey, he had crossed nearly a thousand miles to Kampala, the capital of Uganda. He was now growing stronger in body and wiser in the ways of survival. He remained in Kampala for six months, working at odd jobs and spending every spare moment in the library, reading voraciously.

In that library he came across an illustrated directory of American colleges. One illustration in particular caught his eye. It was of a stately, yet friendly looking institution, set beneath a pure blue sky, graced with fountains and lawns, and surrounded by majestic mountains that reminded him of the magnificent peaks back home in Nyasaland.

Skagit Valley College in Mount Vernon, Washington, became the first concrete image in Legson's seemingly impossible quest. He wrote immediately to the school's dean explaining his situation and asking for a scholarship. Fearing he might not be accepted at Skagit, Legson decided to write to as many colleges as his meager budget would allow.

It wasn't necessary. The dean at Skagit was so impressed with Legson's determination he not only granted him admission but also offered him a scholarship and a job that would pay his room and board.

Another piece of Legson's dream had fallen into place—yet still more obstacles blocked his path. Legson needed a passport and a visa, but to get a passport, he had to provide the government with a verified birth date. Worse yet, to get a visa he needed the round-trip fare to the United States. Again, he picked up pen and paper and wrote to the missionaries who had taught him since childhood. They helped to push the passport through government channels. However, Legson still lacked the airfare required for a visa.

Undeterred, Legson continued his journey to Cairo believing he would somehow get the money he needed. He was so confident he spent the last of his savings on a pair of shoes so he wouldn't have to walk through the door of Skagit Valley College barefoot.

Months passed, and word of his courageous journey began to spread. By the time he reached Khartoum, penniless and exhausted, the legend of Legson Kayira had spanned the ocean between the African continent and Mount Vernon, Washington. The students of Skagit Valley College, with the help of local citizens, sent $650 to cover Legson's fare to America.

When he learned of their generosity, Legson fell to his knees in exhaustion, joy, and gratitude. In December 1960, more than two years after his journey began, Legson Kayira arrived at Skagit Valley College. Carrying his two treasured books, he proudly passed through the towering entrance of the institution.

But Legson Kayira didn't stop once he graduated. Continuing his academic journey, he became a professor of political science at Cambridge University in England and a widely respected author.

Like his heroes, Abraham Lincoln and Booker T. Washington, Legson Kayira rose above his humble beginnings and forged his own destiny. He made a difference in the world and became a magnificent beacon whose light remains as a guide for others to follow.

> ■ **"I learned I was not, as most Africans believed, the victim of my circumstances but the master of them."**
>
> *—Legson Kayira*

UNSTOPPABLE

"Here is the test to find whether your mission on earth is finished: If you're alive, it isn't."

—Richard Bach

.unstoppable.

"Fear not that thy life
shall come to an end,
but rather that it shall
never have a beginning."

—*Cardinal Newman*

UNSTOPPABLE

Homes Are Where Their Hearts Are

Trading a Fortune for a Hammer and a Saw

If the American dream means starting with nothing and accumulating great wealth and assets, then Millard Fuller's story qualifies. But when Millard's dream turned into a nightmare, he decided it was time to redefine his vision.

By the age of thirty, he had earned a million dollars, had the ambition to make $10 million, and possessed the skills and resources to do it. He had a luxurious home, a cabin on a lake, 2,000 acres of land, speed boats, and luxury cars. He also had chest pains and a wife and two young children who seldom saw him because he was always working. His empire was rising, but his marriage and family were crumbling. It happens to thousands of men and women driven in the pursuit of wealth and power. Millard was the one-in-a-million millionaire who had the courage to make a change.

The heart attack hit unexpectedly one day at the office. Not the kind of attack that involves clots and arteries but the kind where grief and regret suddenly flood into your life and your heart metaphorically stands still. It was the day Millard's wife, Linda, announced that she no longer felt she had a husband, that she wasn't sure she loved him anymore, and that she was going to New York City to confer with a minister. Millard was stunned. He had given her everything money could buy. How could Linda not love him?

"The week that followed was the loneliest, most agonizing time in my life," Millard remembered. He began to realize that building his business had cost him everything he truly cared about. This realization was driven home when he watched a movie one night with the line "a planned life can only be endured." A planned life—that's exactly what he was living. But he'd forgotten to include a meaningful purpose in his plan.

He called Linda and begged her to see him. She reluctantly agreed and he immediately caught a plane to meet her in New York. The next few days were filled with tears, an outpouring of their hearts, and a commitment to rebuild their lives on something that mattered. "We both felt a strong sense of God's presence as we talked about the future," Millard explained. "We felt God was calling us to a new way of living." To prepare for this new life, whatever it was, Linda and Millard felt it necessary to get rid of the very things they had allowed to come between them and God in the first place—their business and their material possessions.

They sold everything—the business, the houses, the boats—and donated the proceeds to churches, colleges, and charities. Millard's friends thought he had gone crazy, but Millard had never felt more sane. He was already feeling better. But what to do next?

The answer came during a visit with Clarence Jordan. A theologian in overalls, Clarence had started a Christian community called Koinonia near the small southwest Georgia town of Americus, 140 miles south of Atlanta. Clarence showed Millard the dilapidated shacks that lined the dirt roads of the surrounding countryside. These shanties, which often leaked and lacked heat and plumbing, were homes to hundreds of impoverished families—a scene duplicated countless times throughout the United States and beyond, since 25 percent of the world's population, or 1.38 billion people, live in substandard housing or have no homes at all.

As an expression of their Christian faith, Millard, Clarence, and several co-workers began to build houses for these needy people, one or two at first, then more and more. Sadly, Clarence Jordan died suddenly of a heart attack while the first house was under construction. Millard and his co-workers continued building for four and a half more years in Koinonia.

Moved by the powerful impact that simple but decent houses had on the families that received them, Millard wanted to see if the concepts pioneered in south Georgia would be applicable in other parts of the world. Millard and Linda traveled to Zaire, in central Africa, and in partnership with the Regional Organization of the Protestant Church, successfully built homes throughout the country for three years. Convinced that they had a concept that would work worldwide, they returned to Georgia in 1976 and Millard launched Habitat for Humanity International.

Millard once had a goal to make $10 million. Now he had a new goal. Could he dare believe he could build houses for 10 million people? Why not? Why not more? Millard and Linda saw their mission as a basic, universal truth: "Everyone who gets sleepy at night should have at the very least, a simple, decent, affordable place to lay their heads." Millard believes providing homes is "elemental goodness and love in action—the very essence of true religion."

The idea behind Habitat for Humanity is simple. Initial skeptics called the idea unrealistic, even insane. It is based on no-profit, no-interest loans—something naysayers said was "anti-American and would never work." But Habitat does work. It provides individuals who have inadequate housing and modest income an opportunity, for the first time, to purchase homes with payments they can afford.

To build new homes, Habitat for Humanity relies heavily on volunteers, most of whom have no experience in construction. Cash and materials are donated by various organizations, corporations, and churches. People from all walks of life give their time and skills for free. Yet Habitat is not a charity. The families who benefit from the housing also provide hundreds of hours of sweat equity, building their own homes and the homes of their neighbors. When the new homeowners make the payments on their no-interest, no-profit mortgages, Habitat uses the money to build more homes.

Why have so many people and organizations freely given of themselves to this cause? One reason is that the results are so tangible. So often the world's needs seem too great for one person to make a difference. With Habitat, volunteers work side-by-side with the new homeowners to be. When the house is complete, everyone shares in the pride and joy of the new homeowners.

Habitat for Humanity's goal is to eliminate poverty housing and homelessness everywhere. "I have found that the boldness of goals stirs people, and each year we are amazed at the miracles that come from such boldness," said Millard. With Millard's bold plan, Habitat has already built more than 60,000 houses around the world, providing over 300,000 people with safe, decent, affordable shelter. Habitat for Humanity International has more than 1,400 local affiliates located in all fifty states and more than 250 international affiliates. Habitat coordinates some 800 building programs in fifty-one foreign countries.

But Habitat for Humanity builds more than houses—it builds families, communities, and hope. "Home ownership is often the first step upward in a family and it can break the cycle of despair and futility," explained Millard. "It's reclaimed neighborhoods from drug dealers and squalor with houses that have withstood hurricanes, earthquakes, and floods."

Habitat for Humanity also brings together people from all economic, religious, social, and racial groups. Almost everyone in the United States has seen pictures of former President Jimmy Carter and First Lady Rosalynn Carter decked out in overalls, hammering nails and sawing lumber in the noonday sun. Millard got their support simply by asking them. "I submitted fifteen proposals to the President, hoping he'd agree to at least one or two," Millard said. "To my delight, President Carter agreed to them all."

The Carters are only two of many eminent figures who have joined the cause, lending time, money, and support to Habitat. Hundreds of thousands of other volunteers, eminent in deed only, spend endless hours clearing rubble, hanging drywall, and painting.

By the end of the century, Habitat for Humanity will be the largest homebuilder in the world in terms of the number of homes built. All the mortar and bricks that go into a Habitat house build not just a home, but new lives. It all began because one man and one woman were willing to discard their material riches for something better. Millard and Linda now believe they are two of the richest people alive.

■ **"Our vision to eliminate poverty housing drives us to overcome the numerous obstacles that come in our path. And with God's help, we will achieve our goal, one house at a time."**

—Millard Fuller

.unstoppable.

"Once I asked my counselor for advice about my vocation. I asked, 'How can I know if God is calling me and for what he is calling me?' He answered, 'You will know by your happiness. If you are happy with the idea that God calls you to serve him and your neighbor, this will be the proof of your vocation.'"

—Mother Teresa

▪ UNSTOPPABLE ▪

Exercising Her Vision

In the World of Fitness, She Refused to Think Small

It's a thin world these days—a world of anorexic-looking supermodels, superfit movie stars, and constant reminders that beauty only begins with a size five body.

But some women can't remember *ever* being a size five. For years, they've watched their weight pass the 200- or 300-pound mark and keep climbing. They've given up trying to find clothes that fit. And today's exercise classes, with all their fast stepping and high intensity, are not only impossible to keep up with but humiliating as well.

Sharlyne Powell knows. In 1983 when she was forty-two, she was a size twenty-four and too busy raising a family in Yakima, Washington, to even think about working out. Then she watched her mother die—slowly and painfully—from phlebitis. Sharlyne looked at her twin sons and then looked in the mirror and wondered if she'd just seen her own future. She knew something had to change.

Gathering every bit of courage, Sharlyne walked into a neighborhood aerobics class. Over the next six months, she tried every aerobics class in Yakima. She was *always* the largest person there and could never keep up with the petite instructor who was so flexible she could twist herself into a pretzel. Low-impact aerobics were still years away in 1983, and having no options, Sharlyne decided the only way she would get fit was to start her own class.

"I figured there had to be at least five other women in my town who weren't a size five and who would want to work out as well," she said. Sharlyne borrowed $200 from her husband to rent a hall and went looking for an instructor who wouldn't laugh at her idea and say what everyone else had told her: "Fat women won't exercise. They're too lazy."

When she finally found an instructor who agreed to teach a class, she put a small ad in the newspaper inviting large and extra-large women to come to her first class the following week.

Sixty women showed up.

"I would have been happy if five or six had come," she recalled. When the class had swelled to 150 in two weeks and Sharlyne had to start scheduling two classes a day, she was sure she was on her way.

Two months later, her doors were closed.

"I had made a crucial mistake," she admitted. "I was essentially offering women the same thing the other exercise programs were—the same thin instructors, same style, same everything."

While the classes had been a safe and supportive place for larger women to work out, the exercises were just as intense and just as frustrating. The women had left feeling defeated and disappointed.

To many people, the fact that Sharlyne had to close her doors in two months only confirmed what everyone had told her all along—fat women won't exercise! But Sharlyne didn't believe them. She was convinced large women would exercise if she could offer them something different. "I realized I could either give up my idea or try again and this time do it the way I wanted to in the first place," she said. "I had to learn how to become an instructor myself."

Sharlyne studied everything she could find on exercise and fitness. She attended classes, observed other instructors, then adapted their movements to the needs of a larger body type. Sharlyne and a friend tried out the new exercises themselves. When she and her friend felt ready to teach, Sharlyne reopened the classes at the same hall, naming it the Women at Large Fitness Club.

The first week, 110 women showed up. Two months later, the number was up to 250, and Sharlyne was afraid she would have to start turning away women. She borrowed $10,000 from her husband—this time to buy a rundown, but bigger, 7,000-square-foot building on an acre of land.

Sharlyne's quest for fitness had become a business, and as she and her clients became healthier and slimmer, her business grew. She became determined to become a better instructor and began looking for additional training. That's when she ran into the biggest and most unexpected obstacle she had encountered yet: the fitness industry itself.

She and her instructor friend, who was considerably larger than Sharlyne, had flown to a fitness convention in San Diego, where they had hoped to gain some new skills and begin networking with others in the business.

"People were staring at us like, 'What are *those* people doing here?' It was like we had a bad disease," she remembered. "To them, we did have a disease because we were obese, and it was totally revolting to them."

Sharlyne and her friend had hoped to become certified instructors, but when they approached the certification committee, they were flatly denied. "They said, 'I don't know what you're going to do, Sharlyne; we've never thought of teaching or certifying people like you.'" The words etched themselves into Sharlyne's heart. "I went away angry and heartsick. I thought, if that's the way the fitness professionals treat people like me, we will never be welcome in fitness clubs."

By the time she got home, her depression had turned into determination. She knew there were thousands of women out there just like her who were being ignored not only by the fitness industry, but by every industry. There were women who were tired of having to shop in the men's department just to find a pair of pants and tired of having only brown and black to choose from. There were women who shopped for groceries only after midnight when fewer people would see them and tell cruel jokes behind their backs, making them feel like she and her friend had felt at the fitness convention.

Something had to change, and Sharlyne vowed once again to do everything she could. At her fitness club, she made sure that every woman who walked in the door was treated with warmth and compassion. She created support groups that worked on issues of self-esteem and the feelings of failure that accompany weight problems. She offered special promotions, giving each woman a "heart" for each time she visited the club. As a reward, the woman who collected the most hearts was picked up, along with her husband, by a limousine and taken to a nice hotel where they were treated to dinner and a room for the night. Sharlyne and her crew made sure the room was filled with fresh flowers and the sheets were pulled back and sprinkled with rose petals.

"I wanted to do everything I could to make these women feel special," she said. Her business was so successful that two years after starting Women at Large, Sharlyne decided to franchise. Her research indicated 60 million women in the United States were over their ideal weight. And she had firsthand knowledge of the market, the need, and the solution. By 1987, Women at Large fitness clubs had grown to forty-two locations.

Yet along the way, Sharlyne faced obstacles at every turn. When she saw the need for leotards and tights for larger women, manufacturers laughed in her face. "It would be a waste of money," they told her. "Fat women don't exercise."

So Sharlyne scouted the Pacific Northwest until she found a small, gutsy company in Oregon willing to take the chance. Within a couple of months, Sharlyne's line of large exercise wear brought in more than one-third of her company's income.

She also decided she needed an exercise video to help women who might not live near a Women at Large club or who preferred to work out at home. At that time, Jane Fonda had the only video on the market. Sharlyne took her idea to her club members. Their response was understandable: "You want us to be in a video? *No way!*" She then asked them, if they had had an exercise videotape for large women—before her club opened—would it have helped?

"I had sixty-four women who were willing to put on a leotard in front of a camera and exercise," she said. "We all wore big T-shirts so no one would feel self-conscious."

The distributors in Los Angeles who saw the video weren't enthusiastic. When they all turned her down, Sharlyne decided that, once again, she'd just have to do it herself. She hired a public relations firm to help spread the word about Women at Large; before long, she and the club were featured in magazines and newspapers across the country. The first video sold 50,000 copies. The second video went platinum. A third video followed, and Sharlyne began production on her first infomercial for broadcast on television stations throughout the country.

Although Sharlyne set out to improve herself, she found herself motivated to change the lives of others. "I haven't done anything anybody else can't do if they find something that truly inspires them," she said of her success. "It will require taking some risks and possibly subjecting yourself to ridicule and ignorance. There's always a price. But if you push through, you can go places you never dreamed you could go."

■ **"This has not been just a business, it's been a mission. Because of that, I wasn't about to let anyone stop me from doing what needed to be done for myself and for the other women who came to me for help."**

—Sharlyne Powell

·unstoppable·

"Many persons have the wrong idea about what constitutes true happiness. It is not attained through self-gratification but through fidelity to a worthy purpose."

—Helen Keller

■ UNSTOPPABLE ■

Serious Monkey Business

A Woman Trains Unlikely Soldiers in a War of Independence

In 1977, Mary Joan Willard was making her daily rounds at the Tufts New England Medical Center in Boston. Her work, as part of her fellowship, was to study patients with severe physical injury in rehabilitation. It was there she met a twenty-three-year-old man named Joe.

A car accident had left Joe paralyzed from the neck down. Once active and robust, he now sat helplessly all day in a wheelchair. He couldn't slip a tape into a VCR, fix himself a sandwich, or even lift a finger to scratch a maddening itch. Like more than 100,000 other quadriplegics in the United States, Joe was completely dependent, even for his simplest and most personal needs.

It was this realization that deeply distressed Mary Joan. A woman with enormous self-initiative, she could only imagine how it felt to be trapped by total, permanent dependence. As a psychologist, she knew the emotional cost. Quadriplegics often give up on life, their spirits as paralyzed as their bodies. Mary Joan was convinced that if Joe could achieve some independence, his spirits might again soar.

Lying in bed one evening, a thought came to her—chimpanzees. Why couldn't chimps be trained to do many of the daily tasks to help someone in Joe's position?

The next day Mary Joan visited B. F. Skinner, the Harvard psychologist whose pioneering work with animals and behavior modification had made him world-famous. Mary Joan had worked as Skinner's assistant for three years and she hoped he wouldn't think her idea was crazy.

He didn't. In fact, he thought the idea had merit, but he did offer some caution. Chimps, he reminded her, become much stronger than and grow almost as big as humans. Chimps also have cranky temperaments. He suggested using capuchins instead, the little "organ grinder" monkeys that are intelligent, easy to train, and loyal to their masters. Bingo! Mary Joan was sold.

Next, Mary Joan set out to sell others. After extensive research, she presented her idea to the director of her psychology program at Tufts University. The director almost fell out of his chair laughing. He could just see the headline: "Tufts Medical School Trains Monkeys to Take Care of Patients." Mary Joan wasn't amused and continued with her persuasive argument. Eventually she convinced him the idea was sound and he helped her get a $2,000 grant. This grant was the beginning of an organization called Helping Hands. It was not an auspicious start, but the money was enough to buy four monkeys and some cages and to hire student trainers for a dollar an hour.

Mary Joan's research indicated it would take about eight weeks to train the monkeys. Eight weeks passed and she was still trying to get them out of their cages. The first capuchins, acquired as adults, were former laboratory monkeys and were raised in isolation. Consequently, they were terrified of humans. It took two years of trial and error before Mary Joan had the first monkey ready to begin work.

Despite the frustrating delays, Mary Joan and her new partner, Judi Zazula, worked tirelessly to raise needed funding. Thirty-eight grant proposals resulted in thirty-eight rejections. They were back at square one with Mary Joan working part-time as a psychologist to pay the bills.

Numerous agencies involved with severely disabled persons were interested in her idea, but all were skeptical. Some protested that it was demeaning to quadriplegics to use monkeys as helpers.

"Are Seeing Eye dogs demeaning to the blind?" she responded. Others suggested a mechanical robot would better suit the purpose.

"Can robots sit on your lap and put their arms around you?" she asked.

Other challenges facing Mary Joan and Judi involved training the monkeys to stay out of certain rooms and not get their mischievous little hands into everything. Mary Joan recalled sitting with Judi holding the latest proposal rejection on her lap and watching Hellion, their capuchin-in-training, destroy the place. She said, "Look at this place! To think they almost funded us!" and they both started laughing hysterically.

Mary Joan's patience, determination, and unwavering sense of purpose finally won out. After two years, Hellion, the first trained monkey, was ready to meet a twenty-five-year-old quadriplegic named Robert, who was alone nine hours a day. Hellion could scratch Robert's itchy nose with a face cloth and put a tape in the VCR. She could gently brush his hair, turn the lights on and off, put prepackaged food in the microwave, and even bring Robert a cold drink from the refrigerator. Most important of all, Hellion could pick up Robert's mouth stick, the primary tool a quadriplegic uses for endless tasks, including dialing a telephone, starting a microwave, and turning the pages of a book. Furthermore, Hellion was a devoted companion who entertained Robert and offered unconditional affection.

So successful was the Hellion-Robert team that Mary Joan received her first major grant in 1979 from the Paralyzed Veterans of America. The grant allowed her and Judi to take small salaries, purchase needed equipment, and acquire a few young monkeys for training.

It wasn't long before requests for monkeys came from quadriplegics all across the country. Now the challenge was to find a safe, reliable source of trainable monkeys. Mary Joan and Judi could not continue to use laboratory animals or capuchins caught in the wild; they needed a breeding colony.

Help came from a company that is the symbol of dreams come true—Disney. Disney World in Florida responded to Mary Joan's request and established a capuchin breeding colony on its Discovery Island, supplying Mary Joan's organization with almost all the little "helping hands" it needed. After five years, Disney World needed the space for expansion and provided the funding to move the breeding colony to a Boston zoo.

When they are six to eight weeks old, the monkeys are taken from the colony and placed in volunteer "foster homes." For the next three to five years, they learn basic skills and become comfortable living closely with humans. By the time the monkeys come to Helping Hands, they are housebroken and "cage trained" and have learned upon command to go to their "rooms" and close the door behind them. In the final twelve months of training, the capuchins learn specific skills used in working with quadriplegics, such as combing hair and handling a mouth stick.

This process may seem slow to some, but not to a visionary like Mary Joan Willard. She quickly reminds skeptics that the idea of guide dogs for the blind was debated for a hundred years before the Seeing Eye Program actually began.

By 1997, about 160 capuchins were living in the homes of volunteer families. Thirty-five quadriplegics have received their monkey helpers. Joe, who was Mary Joan's initial inspiration, regained a fair level of motion in his right arm and did not need the help of a monkey. Hundreds of other quadriplegics are not so fortunate and are still patiently waiting for the day when one of Helping Hand's remarkable little monkeys will return to them what they thought they'd lost forever—a little independence, a special form of companionship, and a little joy.

■ **"We both felt that if we did not see this through to the end, no one else would be crazy enough to do it. To give up would have been a disservice to quadriplegics and to ourselves."**

—Mary Joan Willard

.unstoppable.

"Everyone has his own specific vocation in life...Therein he cannot be replaced, nor can his life be repeated. Thus, everyone's task is as unique as is his specific opportunity to implement it."

—Viktor Frankl

UNSTOPPABLE

"I always wanted to be somebody, but I should have been more specific."

--Lily Tomlin

▪ In Their Own Words ▪

***"Some people bring out the best in you** in a way that you might never have fully realized on your own. My mom, Ruby Lloyd Wilson, was one of those people.*

"Most people called her Doll. My father died when I was nine months old, making her a single mother and a widow at the age of eighteen. While I was growing up, there were times when we had so little money that we had to live on a few pounds of dried butter beans for a week at a time. While food was scarce, my mother's love and devotion were abundant. Each night, she sat me on her lap and spoke the words that would change my life, 'Kemmons, you are destined for greatness and you can do anything in life if you're willing to work hard enough to get it.'

"At fourteen, I was hit by a car and the doctors said I would never walk again. My mother took a leave of absence from her job at a meat-packing plant and moved into my hospital room to care for me. Every day, she spoke to me in her gentle, loving voice, reassuring me that no matter what those doctors said, I could walk again if I wanted to badly enough. She drove that message so deep into my heart that I finally believed her. A year later, I returned to school—walking on my own.

"When the Great Depression hit, my mom lost her job like millions of others. I was seventeen, and against Doll's wishes, I left school to support the both of us. At that moment, it became my mission in life to succeed for my mother's sake, and I vowed never to be poor again.

"Over the years, I experienced varying levels of business success. But the real turning point occurred on a vacation I took with my wife and five kids in 1951. I was frustrated at the second-rate accommodations available for families and was furious that they charged an extra $2 for each child. That was too expensive for the average American family, and I was determined to offer them an alternative. I told my

wife that I was going to open a motel for families with a brand name people could trust that never charged extra for children. I figured about 400 nationwide motels would be the right number so that each one would be within a day's drive of about 150 miles. There were plenty of doubters who predicted failure because there wasn't anything remotely similar to this concept at that time.

"Not surprisingly, Doll was one of my strongest supporters and among the first to pitch in. She worked behind the desk and even designed the room decor for the first hundred hotels. As in any business, we experienced enormous challenges. For years, we paid our employees Christmas bonuses with promissory notes because cash was so short. But with my mother's words deeply embedded in my soul, I never doubted we would prevail. Fifteen years later, we had the largest hotel system in the world, with one of the most recognizable names in the business.

"You may not have started out life in the best of circumstances. But if you can find a mission in life worth working for and believe in yourself, nothing can stop you from achieving success."

Kemmons Wilson

Kemmons Wilson founded the first Holiday Inn in 1951 and built it into the largest hotel chain in the world. When he retired in 1979, the company had 1,759 inns in more than fifty countries with annual revenues of $1 billion.

▪ In Their Own Words ▪

"If you can't call the police, who can you turn to? *That's the dilemma I faced eleven years ago when a resident complained to me about officers not responding to calls of violence. After looking further into the complaint, I found a community crying out for help. People had lost pride in their neighborhoods. They'd accepted run-down conditions and the illegal activity taking place on their streets. My heart was moved by their circumstances and I was determined to do something about them.*

"I started with a good old-fashioned cleanup. Working in my off-hours, I organized a picnic in the park, offering a barbecue with all the fixin's to anyone who would help with the cleanup effort. One hundred ninety people showed up and we went to work. We removed abandoned cars, pulled weeds in front of houses, and painted over every speck of graffiti we could find.

"But the drug users and dealers still owned the streets, so I went after them full force. The problem was that ours was a close-knit community, and I was arresting the sons, brothers, friends, and relatives of the same people who were helping me clean up. Sparks flew.

"I received threats on my life. A man was arrested for attempting to kill me. People taunted me on the streets. Someone spray-painted 'Kill Wayne Barton' on a stop sign. They clearly wanted me out of there. But I wasn't about to leave. I felt a strong calling from God, and his message was clear to me: 'Stay focused on your purpose and don't get hung up on the process.' I was there to stay and hoped that over time the people would begin to understand what I was really all about.

"The turning point came during a community meeting when the anger was high. People were demanding that I leave. Then a woman named Miss Jackson stood up and told the crowd, 'I can now go to my mailbox and don't have to sleep on the floor because I'm worried about

a stray bullet hitting me in the head. Until this man came to the community, there was no peace.' After that, a whole wave of people followed with their own testimonies. That meeting turned everything around.

"With the department's support, we opened a study center for the neighborhood children with three paid teachers who tutored from 3:00 P.M. to 7:00 P.M. every day. We opened up computer labs for the kids, developed workshops for parents who wanted to earn their high school equivalency certificates, and provided credit counseling, planning for first-time home buyers, and plenty more. If the community had a problem, I tried to find a cure.

"What a difference a year makes! In time, instead of throwing rocks and bottles at the police, the local residents cheered for us. They tipped us to a violent crime on our new hotline. A sense of community was being restored and people were accepting the responsibility for their role in the change. Why? The payoff was living in a community where the children could play outside without fear. The children have been able to do that now for over ten years.

"When you come across challenges when pursuing a goal, stay focused on your purpose, and remain determined to deal with whatever comes your way. If you hang in there, your sense of purpose will inspire others, and together, you'll be unstoppable!"

Officer Wayne Barton has been a city police officer for seventeen years and has been practicing community policing for ten years in Boca Raton, Florida. He received Parade magazine's 1988 Police Officer of the Year Award and the 1990 Jefferson Award for Outstanding Public Service.

.unstoppable.

"An old man going down a lone highway
Came in the evening cold and gray
To a chasm vast and deep and wide
Through which was flowing a sullen tide.

The old man crossed in the twilight dim;
That swollen stream held no fears for him;
But he turned when safe on the other side
And built a bridge to span the tide.

'Old man,' said a fellow pilgrim near,
'You are wasting your strength with building here;
Your journey will end with the ending day;
You never again must pass this way;
You have crossed the chasm deep and wide—
Why build you this bridge at the eventide?'

The builder lifted his old gray head.
'Good friend, in the path I have come,' he said,
'There followeth after me today
A youth whose feet must pass this way.
This swollen stream which was naught to me
To that fair-haired youth may a pitfall be;
He, too, must cross in the twilight dim;
Good friend, I am building the bridge for him.'"

—Will Allen Dromgoole
THE BRIDGE BUILDER

Your Personal Action Plan

Igniting Purpose in Your Spirit

Purpose can ignite your spirit, providing personal meaning and deep satisfaction to your life. Purpose is the why—why you are here—and your own special calling. Purpose is the unique gifts and insights that you bring to the planet and can contribute to your world. Purpose fuels your efforts and gives you the drive to continue, no matter what the challenges.

If the secret to living a rich, meaningful life is to live in accordance with your purpose, the obvious question remains, How do those who don't know their purpose discover it? It's a difficult but important question, because lasting happiness depends on your ability to answer it truthfully.

William Marsten, a prominent psychologist, asked 3,000 people, "What have you to live for?" The results revealed that 94 percent responded by saying they had no definite purpose for their lives—94 percent! It has been said that "everyone dies, but not everyone really lives." Marsten's survey sadly supports that statement. Too many people live what Thoreau called "lives of quiet desperation"—enduring, waiting, wondering what their lives are all about, hoping their purpose will suddenly become clear to them in a divinely inspired moment. Meanwhile, they simply survive, going through the mechanical motions of living, without ever experiencing the spark of aliveness. They watch their lives quickly pass by and become increasingly fearful that their lives will end before they experience any true joy or deep sense of purpose.

Have you felt that way—that something was missing in your life? I did. For five years I diligently sought to discover what I wanted to do with my life. I was working for a Fortune 500 company and my job brought many rewards including a six-figure income. But I knew that as challenging as my work was, it was not why I was put on the planet.

While working a demanding full-time job, I used my late evenings and weekends to explore other opportunities. I researched several industries and investigated businesses that I could start. I got my real estate license, took courses on importing and exporting, and even helped a friend launch a "home shopping" television show selling art—just to name a few. So what's wrong with this picture? My efforts were scattered. I had no decision-making criteria for the opportunities I investigated. If an opportunity looked interesting and offered strong financial potential, I was interested.

It wasn't until I discovered my true purpose that I experienced genuine direction in my life. Once I had found my purpose, I finally had a guideline to use in evaluating which interests and activities to pursue both personally and professionally.

The entire process, *and it is a process*, didn't occur overnight. The process required self-reflection and patience—two qualities that are difficult for most of us. But now that I've identified my true purpose, it has injected a new-found vitality in my spirit. At the same time, it has provided a sense of peace about my life and where I'm going.

Identifying your true purpose can do the same for you! The following exercises were particularly useful to me in identifying my purpose, and I encourage you to try them.

Step 1: Discover Your Purpose

Action 1: Start by writing "How I Want to Be Remembered." List the qualities, deeds, and characteristics for which you would like to be remembered by your friends, spouse, children, co-workers, the community, and even the world. If you have special relationships with other people or groups, such as a church or synagogue, club, or team, include them on the list too. In the process of writing, you will begin to uncover your true values and the sources of meaning in your life.

To give you an example, I wrote that I wanted to be remembered by my husband as a loving wife who always believed in him, a partner who encouraged him to expand his vision of what was possible and to live his life to its ultimate potential. For my son, I want to be remembered as a mother who deeply loved and believed in him and helped him see that there was no limit to what he could contribute, accomplish, and become if he was committed to achieving it. And my best friend? Guess what? I wanted to be remembered in a similar way.

As I completed this exercise considering other people in my life, a distinct pattern became evident indicating my highest values. Over and over I saw that my purpose, my driving force, was to encourage others. More specifically, my purpose was to encourage individuals to become aware of the greater possibilities for their own lives and to take action to pursue them. Encouraging people is what really excites me and where my natural gifts lie.

Once my purpose became clear, I chose to write this book for my first project. I quit my "day" job and wholeheartedly pursued my chosen path with a passion and a joy that I had never before experienced in any line of "work." Every project that I now pursue is in alignment with my true purpose. As I pursue these projects, I feel alive, invigorated, complete.

According to Peter Drucker (author of *Managing the Non-Profit Organization*), "the question *What do you want to be remembered for?* will induce you to renew yourself; the question makes you see yourself as the person you can become."

As you complete this exercise, observe the patterns that emerge and create your own unstoppable calling. Being clear about your purpose may be your single most important accomplishment.

■ **"The very least you can do in your life is to figure out what you hope for. And the most you can do is live inside that hope. Not admire it from a distance but live right in it, under its roof."**

—Barbara Kingsolver

Action 2: The following chart, provided by authors Mark Victor Hansen and Jack Canfield in *Dare to Win*, is an excellent tool to

	COLUMN I	COLUMN II	COLUMN III
	Describe the *action* you can see yourself doing for others	Describe the *type of person*, *organization*, or *cause* you want to serve	Describe the *goal* you want to co-create with that person, organization, or cause
My purpose in life is to			

help you clarify your purpose. To assist you in completing the chart, I have provided a list of choices for each column. These lists are by no means complete; the intent is to stimulate your thinking about what matters most to you.

Column I: From the following list, choose the actions that best represent your personal calling and most excite you. Write those words in the blanks in Column 1. Chances are you are already engaging in these actions naturally.

ACTIONS

acknowledge	educate	help	praise
advance	elevate	illuminate	promote
alleviate	empower	improve	prepare
assist	encourage	influence	reclaim
build	enroll	inspire	remember
communicate	entertain	instruct	renew
create	explore	liberate	serve
defend	express	listen	strengthen
demonstrate	give	nurture	support
discover	heal	organize	worship

Column II: Below is a brief list of the types of individuals or causes you might be interested in helping. Use this list to prompt your thinking about specific individuals, organizations, or causes that you care about most. Choose one that you would most like to contribute to and write your selection in Column II.

PERSONS, ORGANIZATIONS, AND CAUSES

abused	disadvantaged	physically challenged
at-risk youth	environment	politics environment
animal protection	family issues	poor
bereaved	grass-roots politics	poverty housing
business professionals	homeless	safety
chemically dependent	human rights	senior citizens
children	hunger	teen pregnancy
child protection	immigrants	women
church/synagogue	life-threatening illnesses	women's issues
college students	literacy	veterans
community issues	minorities	youth
crime victims	organ donation	

COLUMN III: The third and final column is for the goal or end result you want to create for the individual, group, or cause. This goal should be a core value, ideal, or issue that is so important, you are willing to dedicate your time and resources to make it happen.

GOALS

acceptance	health/vitality	self-confidence
faith	safety	enjoyment
leaving a legacy	being capable	living responsibly
achievement	independence	self-esteem
freedom	security	equality
love	competency	living life to its fullest
being the best	joy	self-sufficiency
growth	self-actualization	excellence
making a contribution	dignity	learning
believing in themselves	justice	serving others

Here are some examples of filled-in charts:

	Column I	Column II	Column III
My purpose in life is to	instruct	at-risk youths	raise self-esteem
My purpose in life is to	educate	the *public* (who) on the importance of organ donations (cause)	enable people's lives to be saved
My purpose in life is to	support	individuals with physical challlenges	develop their independence
Cynthia Kersey's purpose in life is to	encourage, inspire, and instruct	people from all walks of life	enable them to become aware of the greater possibilities for their own lives and to take action

I hope by now you are beginning to have a better understanding of your unique calling. Most people find that defining their purpose is an evolutionary process that is fine-tuned over a period of time. It certainly was for me.

But consider the return on your investment. Once you determine where you're headed and why, you could potentially save years of wasted time by not pursuing activities and vocations that offer little meaning and lack harmony with your true sense of purpose. Life is too short to spend it on anything less than meaningful activities.

Once you have awakened to your purpose, no obstacle will be able to stop you. It's simply too important! You will emerge happier, stronger, and healthier, for purpose ignites the spirit and heals the soul.

■ **"Make no little plans; they have no magic to stir men's blood... Make big plans...aim high in hope and work."**

—Daniel H. Burnham, Chicago Architect and Planner

Step 2: Integrate Purpose into Your Daily Life

Once you have a clearly defined purpose, you now know where to focus your energies and efforts. Now you can begin to establish goals and make plans—goals and plans that serve your purpose and help create a life of greater meaning. Present and future goals should be evaluated by one criterion only: Do the goals serve your purpose?

To have purpose in life doesn't mean you have to quit your job, give away your material possessions, and join a mission in Calcutta—unless that's your true desire. You can live "on purpose" no matter what your vocation. Officer Wayne Barton's story is a great example. He is employed as a police officer, but his job is only part of his much broader sense of purpose to make a difference in his community. His goals and activities, on and off the job, are focused on serving that purpose.

Action: Identify one way you can integrate purpose into your life—through your job, business, or community. For example, let's say your purpose emerges as a desire to serve your community. Whatever your vocation—domestic, artistic, business, or otherwise—your next step could be to:

- Sign up for that committee you've been saying no to
- Volunteer one day per month to serve someone else
- Mentor a new employee at work

- Become a Big Brother or Big Sister
- Support Love Letters by writing to children with serious illnesses
- Join Habitat for Humanity and help build a home for a family in need
- Teach someone how to read
- Take the extra step "above and beyond" to provide services to a customer or find a solution to a problem outside your job description

Commit yourself to taking action this week. Make that phone call. Soon, your goals will start taking shape and every aspect of your life will reflect and serve your purpose. When that happens, you will have a power to overcome obstacles that you have never experienced before.

■ **"There is no failure
except in no longer trying.
There is no defeat except from within,
no really insurmountable barrier
save our own inherent weakness of purpose."**

—Elbert Hubbard

Characteristic Two

PASSION
Fuels Inexhaustible Energy

When purpose ignites the spirit, it generates an inexhaustible fire that burns in the heart of every unstoppable person. That fire is passion and it is vividly demonstrated by those whom you are about to meet in this chapter.

If you met them in person, you would see the passion in their eyes, hear it in their voices, and feel it in their presence. Passion fueled their energy; it provided the momentum to plow through frustrations and challenging times and supplied the joy when external rewards were scarce.

Are you passionate about your life? Do you love what you do? Are you pursuing a career and goals that fuel you with inexhaustible energy and enthusiasm? If the answer is no, don't despair. After reading the stories, "Your Personal Action Plan" will reveal how to identify your passion and create ways to integrate it into your everyday life and career.

By living on purpose and pursuing dreams and goals that are consistent with your natural strengths and desires, you can create unstoppable passion almost effortlessly. And when that happens, *nothing* can stop you!

■ **"You have to find something that you love enough to be able to take risks, jump over the hurdles, and break through the brick walls that are always going to be placed in front of you. If you don't have that kind of feeling for what it is you're doing, you'll stop at the first giant hurdle."**

—George Lucas

■ UNSTOPPABLE ■

Rising from the Rubble

It Would Take a Miracle—So He Found One

There were few things in the world that Francisco Bucio wanted more than the fulfillment of his desire—to be a surgeon.

At the age of twenty-seven, Francisco seemed well on his way to achieving that dream. His skill had earned him a residency in plastic surgery at Mexico City's General Hospital, and in only a few more years he'd be able to establish a private practice. Then, on September 19, 1985, Francisco's world crashed down around him.

An earthquake, one of the largest in history, measuring 8.1 on the Richter Scale, claimed more than 4,200 lives. What could not be measured was the toll the earthquake took on human dreams.

When the tremors started, Francisco was in his room on the hospital's fifth floor. When the tremors ended, he was on the ground floor, buried under tons of debris. In total darkness, as he listened to the dying gasps of his roommate, Francisco realized his right hand—the one with which he performed surgery—was crushed under a massive steel beam. As Francisco struggled painfully and frantically, unable to pull his hand free, he started to panic. As a doctor, he knew that without circulation, his hand would turn gangrenous, and if that happened, the hand would have to be amputated.

As the hours passed, Francisco drifted in and out of consciousness, growing weaker and weaker. But outside the building, the determination that runs in the Bucio family was making its mark. His father and six brothers joined countless volunteers digging frantically in the rubble with picks and shovels. His family never lost hope. Four days later, they finally reached Francisco.

Professional rescuers at the scene said they would have to cut off Francisco's hand to free him. His family, aware of Francisco's dream of becoming a surgeon, refused. Instead, the rescue team worked three more hours with a crane to lift the beam crushing Francisco's hand. Once Francisco was freed, they rushed him to another hospital. In the months that followed, while Mexico struggled to rebuild its capital, Francisco Bucio struggled to rebuild his dream.

The first step was an eighteen-hour operation that surgeons hoped would save Francisco's damaged hand. But as days passed, Francisco's hope dimmed. Nerves in his fingers failed to regenerate, and after three weeks, doctors were forced to amputate four fingers, leaving only Francisco's thumb. By then, Francisco had steeled himself for what lay ahead; his goal now was to save what was left of his right hand. Over the next few months, he underwent five more operations. Still his hand would not function. Without his right hand, how could he operate on patients? Francisco set out in search of a miracle.

His quest led him to San Francisco and Dr. Harry Buncke, Chief of Microsurgery at Davies Medical Center. Dr. Buncke had pioneered the transplantation of toes to replace missing fingers. Francisco realized that Dr. Buncke was probably his last hope and promised himself, *If Dr. Buncke can successfully complete the operation, I'll take care of the rest.*

In the surgery, Dr. Buncke replaced Francisco's ring and pinkie fingers with two of his toes. After time and hard work, Francisco was able to grasp objects between his thumb and two "fingers." This enabled him to do simple tasks like buttoning his clothes. After recuperating from the complex surgery, Francisco threw himself full force into an intensive therapy and exercise program. He spent painful hours placing pegs into pegboards, then laboring with a pencil and pad until he could sign his name perfectly. Dr. Buncke assured him, "A hand rehabilitates itself to its own need. If the needs are great, the skills become great."

After several months of dedicated rehabilitation, Francisco returned to Mexico City where he performed limited duties at the hospital and continued to train like an Olympic athlete. He swam for conditioning and, to strengthen his hand, practiced tying and untying thousands of knots, suturing with needles on clothes, dicing food into tiny pieces, and rolling rubber balls between his new fingers. In the beginning, completing even the simplest movements was awkward and frustrating. But Francisco persisted until he was able to perform each task with precision. He worked his left hand too, training himself to be ambidextrous.

Then came the day when Francisco faced his most critical test.

A senior resident had been watching Francisco progress from cleaning and wrapping wounds to executing simple surgical procedures like removing moles. He asked Francisco to assist in an operation on a man with a broken nose. The procedure was extremely delicate, and Francisco assumed he would simply pass the instruments. But as the resident prepared to remove cartilage from the man's rib for use in rebuilding the nose, he turned to Francisco and said, "You get the cartilage."

It was Francisco's moment of truth and he knew it. The success of this procedure would mean his return to surgery—or a devastating setback. Taking courage in hand—both hands—he painstakingly removed the cartilage. What would have been done by another surgeon in ten minutes took Francisco one hour, but it was an hour of triumph. Later in describing the event, he said, "This procedure required a lot of skill and when I did it, I realized I could do anything!"

Today, Francisco Bucio is a highly regarded plastic surgeon practicing at two locations in Tijuana and offering a full range of services. He also volunteers his time working with the poor, correcting the cleft palates of children and performing reconstructive surgery on young burn victims. "Having had six operations of my own," he said, "I can empathize with my patients—I know how it feels to be afraid."

Some people have affectionately called him the "surgeon who operates with his feet." Francisco doesn't mind. With a smile, he replied, "My hand may not look pretty, but it works just fine. It is the miracle that allows me to do the work I most love and to give something back to those who now need miracles of their own."

■ **"We all face obstacles of one kind or another in life. But if you let your deepest passion serve as your fuel, you'll be able to travel the road back and move on to make your dreams happen."**

—Dr. Francisco Bucio

Choose something you love to do.

·unstoppable·

"Only passions,
great passions,
can elevate the soul
to great things."

—*Diderot*

UNSTOPPABLE

Inside Every Daydream Was a Hollywood Script

Passion Paved the Way

It was clear from the start that Stephen J. Cannell would never amount to much. In school, he was still struggling to learn to read when his classmates had moved on to much more advanced skills. In response, the teachers did what they usually did in the 1950s—they flunked him. They flunked him in first grade, at the delicate age when children begin to develop their sense of self-worth and potential. They flunked him again in fourth grade and this time asked him to leave school—a privilege they could freely exercise because the school was private. Next for Stephen was a remedial school, where the staff attributed his reading difficulty to weak eyesight. Never mind that Stephen had 20/20 vision; he was forced for an hour each day to complete tedious eye exercises.

It wasn't any better when he enrolled at a prestigious private high school in Connecticut. He flunked tenth grade there and was asked, once again, to leave. Transferring to yet another school, Stephen repeated tenth grade and eventually graduated at the bottom of his class.

Years after these demoralizing experiences, at the age of thirty-five, Stephen discovered he had dyslexia—a learning disability in no way related to intelligence. Today, dyslexia can be identified and treated with early intervention. When Stephen was in school, however, children with dyslexia were often labeled "slow" and "stupid." Many years before Stephen, three other dyslexic youths no doubt suffered the same humiliation. They were Albert Einstein, Thomas Edison, and Hans Christian Andersen.

One would assume that Stephen's academic career would have left him with no self-esteem and even less ambition. But he had several things going for him: athletic success in football and track; a supportive father, who had experienced his own academic frustrations early in life and later discovered he suffered from the same learning disorder as his son; and an imagination as rich as his grades were poor.

And what an imagination! While other students struggled for grades and awards, Stephen stared out the window and daydreamed. His father called him the "Storyteller" because he always created stories to entertain other children. Stephen's reading was slow and his recall was weak, but his imagination was quick and powerful.

In 1961, a football scholarship brought him to the University of Oregon; he later lost the scholarship because of his poor grades. While at the university, Stephen met Ralph Salisbury, an encouraging creative writing professor, who taught him how to transform fantasy into the written word. From that experience, Stephen decided to become a professional writer—an interesting choice for someone who flunked almost all of his English courses. "Since I was the dumbest kid in class, being perfect on paper never entered my mind. I always wrote to entertain myself, which made it easier—it took the pressure off."

After completing his education, Stephen reluctantly went to work in the family business (interior design and decorating). But he had no interest in the business. When he came home at night, he sat at his typewriter and wrote stories. One hour after work became two hours. Before long, Stephen was spending at least four hours every night typing out short stories, television and movie plots, and other material produced by his vivid imagination.

"Deep down," he said, "I figured I wasn't the brightest guy around. But my attitude was always, who cares? I won't think about that today." Stephen had identified a vocation he really loved, and where there is passion, there is little room for doubt.

His writing career began in 1966 when he sold a script for a television series called *Adam 12*. Since that first script sale, he has created or co-created more shows than anyone in television history, including major network hits such as *The Rockford Files*, *Baretta*, *The A-Team*, *Hunter*, *Riptide*, *Wiseguy*, and *The Commish*. Stephen also became the largest independent producer of prime-time television shows and has received a number of Emmy Awards. Eventually he established his own studio, which has since surpassed the $1 billion production mark. He is now working on his third novel and has several new television shows on the air and in development.

Stephen still remembers his astonishment when the reviewer of an early show called him "brilliant…an up-and-coming genius." It had never occurred to Stephen that he was brilliant. However, he had been blessed with an understanding and supportive father and mother who had encouraged him to pursue his passion and realize his dreams. Stephen today refers to his father as his best friend and mentor and keeps his father's photograph on his office wall.

Stephen J. Cannell not only overcame the challenge of dyslexia but also has used it to his advantage. Many of his most appealing characters are outsiders, nonconformists like himself. He feels his early disappointments in life helped him develop a valuable resiliency and a drive to "push forward" in business. Above all, the world of imagination and fantasy he developed as his refuge in his youth became the fertile world he has mined for so many of his ideas as a television writer and novelist.

Stephen's passion to share those ideas and stories with the world—to succeed at doing what he loves most—transformed the flunking student into one of the most successful figures in the television industry.

> ■ **"Doing something I really love has served my career more than anything else, except for my wife and family."**
>
> *—Stephen J. Cannell*

·unstoppable·

"Make sure that the career you choose is one you enjoy. If you don't enjoy what you're doing, it will be difficult to give the extra time, effort, and devotion it takes to be a success. If it is a career that you find fun and enjoyable, then you will do whatever it takes. You will give freely of your time and effort and you will not feel that you are making a sacrifice in order to be a success."

—Kathy Whitworth, Professional Golfer

■ UNSTOPPABLE ■

She Gave New Shape to the Shoe Business

Then She Added the Soul

Why not?

That's what Sheri Poe kept asking herself when she and her friends came out of exercise class with backaches and sore feet because their shoes were all wrong. Sheri did some research and discovered that women's athletic shoes were only scaled-down versions of men's shoes, although the female foot is shaped differently. She and her husband, Martin Birrittella, had been looking for the right business to start and thought, *why not*. Why not start a company that manufactures athletic shoes specifically designed for a woman's foot? Shoes that *fit*.

People were more than willing to tell Sheri and Martin why not. For one thing, the couple had no capital and no experience in the industry. Experts said it was sheer lunacy to think anyone could compete against Nike and Reebok, huge companies that dominated the athletic shoe market. Besides, neither Sheri nor Martin had a college degree. Sheri's education had been cut short after she'd been raped in her freshman year. The traumatic event was followed by years of bulimia, hepatitis, and other health problems stemming from the attack. Sheri's dedication to fitness helped her through the healing process. Having conquered the biggest obstacle—recovering from such a degrading physical assault—Sheri knew she could meet the challenge of creating the perfect fitness shoe for women.

First, she did her own footwork. Posing as a graduate student, she spent months interviewing hundreds of customers and shoe salesclerks. Her research confirmed a real need for women's athletic shoes.

For seed money, Sheri and her husband took a third mortgage on their modest home and borrowed from friends, family, and anyone else who shared their enthusiasm for the project. Then they went to venture capitalists for serious financing. "The reactions were always the same," recalled Sheri. "They said it was insane to think we could break into this market having no experience within this industry and create a new brand in such a competitive field. They suggested we take the idea to Nike or Reebok and forget about doing it ourselves.

"We started Rykä because we knew the demand was great and no one was addressing the need. We dreamed of one day seeing our shoes on aerobics instructors, in retail stores, and having a booth at a big convention right next to Nike and Reebok. It was a picture so exhilarating that any negativity I heard didn't even matter."

Still, it wasn't easy. Their dream required an enormous financial investment, and venture capitalists suggested the best way to raise the money was to take their new company public. After several months, Sheri and Martin found an investment banker who thought the idea of "shoes made by women for women" was a hot one. The banker loaned them $250,000 and gave them a letter of intent to go public in the spring of 1988. Sheri and Martin were finally on their way.

They say timing is everything, but time didn't seem to be on Sheri and Martin's side. Just as they were about to go public, the stock market crashed. "I was in shock," Sheri remembered. "How were we supposed to pull off an initial public offering right after a crash?" They expected a call from their banker asking for the money back. Instead the banker called the next day to say there was still a tremendous amount of interest in Rykä and they were going to move forward with the initial public offering.

Rykä, Inc., went public five months later. The offering raised $4 million in stock before Rykä had shipped a single shoe. The future looked bright indeed. Sheri and Martin's undying passion and commitment enabled them to overcome a major hurdle. In the following months, they would need that commitment.

The first pair of specially ordered shoes arrived and Sheri put them on. Her heart sank. The shoes were nothing like the ones they had designed! The manufacturer had mistakenly used the wrong foot form and had simply made a smaller version of a man's shoe. The whole point of their enterprise had been lost, and thousands of the shoes had already shipped to retailers nationwide.

Sheri acted quickly. She contacted key retailers and buyers and explained the production problem. The stores returned the shoes and Sheri had the shoes re-made according to the original specifications.

Rykä was back in business but had missed an entire season of selling. The loss of time was a major setback. Sheri knew she had better get the word out about her new product—and fast. With limited funds, she designed a program for the women who could be walking billboards for her product—aerobics instructors. She offered her shoes to the instructors at a discount, then challenged them to put her shoes to the test. After wearing the shoes, the aerobics instructors immediately experienced a difference. They spread the word about Rykä shoes, and a grassroots movement developed.

It was time to expand her reach even further and another *why not?* occurred to Sheri. In 1987, there were almost no women executives in the athletic footwear industry. Sheri wanted to capitalize on her uniqueness, and since Rykä could not afford a national advertising campaign, she came up with an alternative plan: Sheri took her story to the media. She hired an inexpensive public relations firm and sent a pair of shoes and a letter telling the Rykä story to the editors of key magazines and newspapers. Her strategy worked. Within a year, Sheri was featured in *Entrepreneurial Woman* and *Working Woman* and in dozens of articles in trade publications for the sporting goods industry.

One notable woman to whom Sheri sent her package was Oprah Winfrey. Every few months Sheri sent boxes of shoes and T-shirts to Oprah and her staff, hoping to get their attention. One day the phone rang. Oprah's producer was calling to invite Sheri to be on Oprah's show. "I was so shocked," Sheri remembered, "that I turned white and could barely breathe." The producer said Sheri had not originally been on Oprah's list, but during a staff meeting, they were considering various female entrepreneurs for an upcoming show, and Oprah noticed the boxes of Rykä shoes stacked in a corner of the room. "I know," Oprah had suggested, "what about our Rykä woman?"

Sheri's appearance on the show was the chance to show off her innovative footwear to a nationwide audience of millions of women viewers. Within weeks, all of Rykä's shoes sold out, and the company had no stock to replace them. What should have been a business bonanza became a setback that took Rykä three months to recover from while Sheri reorganized her company to meet the demand.

Years later came another unexpected break in the form of England's Princess Diana. Reading about Princess Diana's public confession of her battle with bulimia, Sheri acted on impulse and wrote the princess a letter to express sympathy and share her own story. Sheri wrote not as a fan, or as a shoe manufacturer, but as a fellow survivor. To ensure that the letter reached Diana's desk, Sheri asked her distributor in the United Kingdom to find out the name of Princess Diana's trainer. A package was sent to the trainer and she agreed to deliver the note and a pair of shoes to the princess. Sheri's letter yielded unexpected rewards. In every photograph Sheri saw of Diana during the next three months, the princess was wearing Rykäs.

Women around the world also saw those Rykäs and began buying the shoes in increasing numbers. In 1994, Rykä's sales reached an all-time high of $15 million. Yet for all her success, Sheri felt the real soul of the company was missing. "We are a company that sells products solely to women. I felt a need to contribute on a corporate level to women's well-being. I had always felt that if my company became profitable, I wanted to make a difference."

Realizing that domestic violence had become the leading cause of injury to women, Sheri founded Regaining One's Self-Esteem (ROSE), a separate, nonprofit foundation that funds shelters, education programs, and rape crisis centers. Additionally, each pair of Rykä shoes carries a tag offering women tips on how to be safe and what to do if attacked.

Sheri Poe gave the sporting goods industry a wake-up call about the importance of the women's market. Since then, the women's athletic footwear industry has grown into a $5 billion industry. Rykä, now merged with Global Sports, Inc., continues to sell shoes designed especially for women's feet. Sheri remains founder and spokesperson for Rykä and is now pursuing another entrepreneurial passion, developing children's products.

Thanks to Sheri Poe's passion and determination, women can now work out in shoes that fit their needs. Even more importantly, the sales of those shoes mean that thousands of abused women are safer and more confident.

Why not?

■ **"I believe the reason that we were able to do this was because we saw a need in the market, had incredible passion, and were committed to making it happen. Our enthusiasm was totally infectious, and we found people who wanted to help us."**

—Sheri Poe

"OUR LOAN OFFICERS ARE CONSIDERING YOUR APPLICATION NOW, MADAM."

.unstoppable.

"The most powerful weapon on earth is the human soul on fire."

—Marshall Foch

■ UNSTOPPABLE ■

Dancing to the Rhythms of Her Heart

An Unfulfilled Professional Finds a Bigger Stage

Maybe it was the ticking clock in her office. Maybe it was the nagging voice in her head that couldn't be silenced as the years kept passing.

Whatever it was, it all came down to one day in Robyn Allan's life when she decided to leave her office at the official closing time, climb into a cab, and do what she wanted to do more than anything else in life—dance.

"I swore to myself that I would get in that cab no matter what, ride away, and start taking dance lessons again. In the cab, I felt terribly guilty about leaving on time instead of working late as I usually did. But the next time I did it, it was easier. And it got easier and easier after that."

Robyn was a successful economist and held a high position in a major Canadian financial institution in Vancouver. She had two great kids and a lovely home. But something was missing; she felt incomplete. From the age of sixteen, when she had taken her first dance class, she had passionately wanted to be a dancer. And though she had studied dance off and on, and performed semiprofessionally, she had never shown the kind of talent necessary to really succeed. Business had come more easily. She got a master's degree in economics and built a successful career.

"I had been taught by my parents that you do what you can do well, and if you can't be excellent at something, don't do it. Since I had a passion for dance but did not have the talent for greatness, there has always been an incredible love/hate struggle within me about whether or not I should continue."

Heeding the words of her parents and conforming to what she felt society expected of her, Robyn buried her passion and devoted herself to her family and career. Yet she never stopped daydreaming about producing and performing in a full-length dance theater production, all the while convincing herself that she lacked the time, ability, creativity, and money to do it successfully.

Then came the day when she had a frightening vision while she was sitting in her office. She was thirty-two years old but saw herself as an old woman, no longer able to dance on stage, looking back on a life of unrealized dreams. At that moment, she felt a surge of resolve—she would create a show, even if people laughed at her, even if she danced alone in a theater with empty seats. That was the day she jumped into a cab and returned to her dance lessons with unshakable determination.

Passion and commitment have a way of making good things happen. Within days of Robyn's decision, a friend brought her an article about Andravy Mayes, a choreographer and performer from Los Angeles who would be teaching in nearby White Rock. Robyn hesitated, then worked up the courage to call him. "It was like magic—we met, and the next thing I knew we were working on my dream."

Together, in their off-hours, Robyn and Andravy wrote *Don't Break the Glass*, a musical comedy about a woman coming to terms with her place on the stage and in life. They choreographed the dance pieces, took leads in the performance, and assembled a cast of actors and dancers for the remaining parts. Andravy was just the teacher and partner Robyn needed. "He knew how to highlight my strengths and make me look good, the way a skilled photographer gives someone the right light or camera angle. He knew as a dancer what I could work with and what I couldn't."

Although Andravy knew how to emphasize Robyn's strengths, she found the work extremely challenging. The production required total commitment and perseverance, even when it wasn't going as well as she wanted, even when it *hurt*. As Robyn got more and more rehearsals under her belt, she eventually experienced a breakthrough and everything came together.

Robyn's biggest surprise was discovering she did not have to sacrifice all other areas of her life to pursue her dream. "I had always believed if you do something requiring a lot of effort, other things suffer, like your kids or career. What actually happened was that I became more productive and achieved greater results at work than ever before. I had a renewed confidence and sense of self that was reflected in my work. I was also a lot more fun and spontaneous around my kids. They participated with me in the show, taking tickets, working the lights, and they loved it. The time we spent together as a family was better, much better."

Seven months after her first meeting with Andravy, *Don't Break the Glass* opened successfully in Vancouver. It was so well received Robyn and Andravy extended the run by taking the production to White Rock. "People related to the story line. So many have desires they never fulfilled. And so many miss the opportunity to discover a vast treasure of self-discovery—the dance between who they are and who they can become."

Robyn continued with both careers, in the office and on the stage. She went on to serve as president and CEO of the Insurance Corporation of British Columbia, Canada's largest insurer. Now, as president of her own company, she is a much sought-after business consultant and speaker. Yet Robyn still has found time to produce, choreograph and perform in four dance shows that have played to large audiences and rave reviews. Robyn Allan completed her life by listening to the music in her heart.

■ "Many of us are afraid to follow our passions, to pursue what we want most because it means taking risks and even facing failure. But to pursue your passion with all your heart and soul is success in itself. The greatest failure is to have never really tried."

—Robyn Allan

unstoppable.

"I would rather be a failure doing something I love than be a success doing something I hate."

—*George Burns*

▪ In Their Own Words ▪

***"Without a doubt, one attribute that** has contributed greatly to what I've accomplished is my enthusiasm. I am not afraid to get excited about things, and I've found that passion is contagious.*

"This attitude has worked for me not just in the entertainment business but with projects designed to help others. Often these have been far more rewarding than my personal or career successes. One of those nonprofit projects was Hands Across America, which I produced in 1986. The inspiration came from the USA for Africa We Are the World campaign, in which dozens of top musicians and singers gathered to record a song that raised $60 million to feed African families suffering from the famine there. From my involvement as organizer of We Are the World, I developed the idea of creating a human chain across America on Memorial Day 1986 that would send a message about our commitment to solving the problems of the hungry and homeless. As crazy as it sounds, I envisioned millions of people holding hands to form an unbroken line of humanity, spanning more than 4,000 miles across seventeen states.

"When I first started discussing the idea, people thought it was fantastic—but also logistically impossible. Frankly, I didn't know exactly how I would pull it off, either. But I was so excited about it, I had complete faith that it would happen. I took my enthusiasm to Sergio Zyman, marketing vice president of the Coca-Cola Company, and convinced him to put up $5 million to help make Hands a reality. With that seed money, we started organizing and promoting the event and quickly found out how daunting a challenge we'd taken on. We had to work through endless red tape to get clearances from community to community—the insurance alone cost us $3 million. The media took potshots at the idea from the start, and Hands Across America became the subject of standup comedy jokes. I even gave up sitting in window seats on

airplanes to avoid looking down at those endless miles of land that we would have to somehow fill with people.

"Every day, I flew to three or four different cities, giving speeches and television interviews, trying to stir up volunteers. Yet with less than two months to go before the May 25 event, we had fewer than a million people signed up, less than 20 percent of what we knew we needed. So we kept going, promoting the event and encouraging America to join in.

"On Memorial Day 1986, 5.5 million men, women, and children of every race, creed, and color turned out to join hands. In addition to raising $34 million, Hands Across America became the single biggest participatory event in history, a symbol of hope and generosity witnessed by an additional hundreds of millions of people around the world.

"If you want to achieve great things in your life, you have to take risks. The first risk is daring to feel deeply, to be passionate about what you want and care about. Enthusiasm is the key to breaking through barriers, whether your dream is to touch one person or millions."

Ken Kragen is one of Hollywood's most respected and successful personal managers and producers, handling such clients as Kenny Rogers, Travis Tritt, Trisha Yearwood, and Lionel Richie.

▪ In Their Own Words ▪

***"Early on I decided not to allow the** opinions of others to stop me from pursuing my passion to become a musician. I grew up on a farm in northeast Scotland and began taking piano lessons when I was eight. The older I got, the more my passion for music grew. But I also began to gradually lose my hearing. Doctors concluded that irreversible nerve damage was the cause and by age twelve, I was profoundly deaf. But my love for music never left me.*

"My goal was to become a percussion soloist, even though there were none at that time. To perform, I learned to 'hear' music differently from others. I play in my stocking feet and can tell the pitch of a note by the vibrations I feel through my body and through my imagination. My entire sound world exists by utilizing almost every sense that I have.

"I was determined to be assessed as a musician, not as a deaf musician, and I applied to the prestigious Royal Academy of Music in London. No other deaf student had done this before and some teachers opposed my admission. Based on my performance, I was finally admitted and went on to graduate with the academy's highest honors.

"After that, I established myself as essentially the first full-time solo percussionist. I wrote and arranged numerous musical compositions since few had been written expressly for solo percussionists.

"I have been a soloist for over ten years because I decided early on that just because my doctor made a diagnosis that I was profoundly deaf, it didn't mean that my passion couldn't be actualized. I would encourage people to not allow themselves to be defined or

limited by others. Follow your passion; follow your heart. They will lead you to the place you want to go."

Evelyn Glennie is renowned as the first lady of solo percussion. She performs 120 concerts each year and has recorded nine albums.

Your Personal Action Plan

Energizing Your Passion

Passion generates a supply of positive energy far more abundant than vitamins, exercise, or any other health remedy you can imagine. When you're passionate about what you do, it's not just the destination that matters, but the entire journey. From beginning to end, the journey is an adventure.

When you love what you do, you have the energy to overcome any obstacle. Doing what you love has three immediate benefits:

1. You'll be highly motivated.

Passion is the fuel that drives you. It is an inexhaustible resource for energy and optimism.

> ■ **"When you're passionate, you're focused, purposeful, and determined, without even having to try. Your body, mind, and spirit are all working in unison towards the same goal."**
>
> —*Marcia Wieder, Author of* Making Your Dreams Come True

Without passion, it's nearly impossible to sustain the high level of energy and interest you need to be unstoppable. In fact, without passion, one simply reduces life to existence, mediocrity, and indifference.

The choice is yours. You can choose to access your lifeblood by getting in touch with your purpose and pursuing activities that ignite your passion. Or you can choose to be like too many others who trudge through life in a state of endurance, missing most of what they experience. Such people observe life but don't experience its pleasure. If life were a symphony, they would hear the notes, but miss the genius behind the composition. If life were a rare gem, they would see the color, but pay no attention to the intricacies of the cut. If life were a novel, they would understand the plot, but overlook the subtle images and symbolism.

To live without passion is to live without fully experiencing life's wonder, drama, and excitement. Living with passion allows you to experience your senses to their fullest.

Passion is the energy that will propel you through any obstacle and turn your dreams into reality.

2. Work will seem like play.

People with passion find it difficult to use the word "work." Such people are pursuing what they most enjoy and what is personally rewarding. Everyone is born with a limited amount of time. Every moment we live—whether we're working, playing, complaining, or being thankful—is time that we've spent. Nothing is more valuable than the time we have left. When we're pursuing our passion, it isn't just getting to the goal, because the journey is as rewarding as the end result. At the end of our lives we can say, "I've loved my life"—the ultimate definition of success.

3. Others will share your passion and enthusiasm.

Enthusiasm draws like a magnet, attracting others to your cause. Sometimes, other people are not even sure why they've joined up. Their logic tells them no, yet instinctively they say yes. It's been said that nothing sells like passion; the experiences you've just read about in this chapter prove the truth of that statement.

Despite Sheri Poe's lack of experience in a highly competitive industry, she and her husband were able to take their start-up company public by convincing an investment banker that the idea of "shoes made by women for women" was a hot one. Ken Kragen created the single largest participatory event *in history* and raised $34 million for the homeless by persuading 5.5 million men, women, and children to join a human chain spanning 4,000 miles. How did Sheri and Ken accomplish their goals? The passion of their words and their very being inspired people to support their cause. People simply couldn't resist their enthusiasm.

Cosmetic giant Mary Kay Ash said, "A mediocre idea that generates enthusiasm will go further than a great idea that inspires no one." Your passion is an asset. Use it to inspire and enlist the support of others. People ultimately have no choice but to honor passionate commitment.

> ■ **"You can't sweep other people off their feet if you can't be swept off your own."**
>
> —*Clarence Day*

Step 1: Identify Your Passion

To instill passion in your life, you must first return to your purpose. Purpose can lead you down many different paths. Let your unique personality, desires, and natural strengths lead you to the path that is right for you. The following exercises will assist you in finding that path.

Action 1: Determine what you love. Ken Kragen calls it a "Personal Balance Sheet" in *Life Is a Contact Sport*. Barbara Winter calls it "Uncovering Your Assets" in *Making a Living Without a Job*. Hopson & Scally, authors of *Build Your Own Rainbow*, call it a "Personal Characteristics Inventory." All are effective tools for determining what you love to do. Regardless of what you call it, the key is to realistically assess, based on where you are today, what you love to do and the assets you bring to the table. I suggest that you pull out a pen and paper again and list in separate columns your *likes and dislikes*, your *strengths and areas needing improvement*. Take special notice of your likes and strengths. They hold the key to what you would be most passionate about in life.

Here is an example of my list *prior* to starting this project:

LIKES	DISLIKES
Learning	Listening to negative people/whiners
Asking questions	Engaging in small talk
Undertaking challenging, multifaceted projects	Managing lots of employees
Encouraging others	Giving people bad news; e.g., firing or rejecting them
Reading books	Doing paperwork
Brainstorming	Dealing with office or company politics

LIKES *(cont')*	DISLIKES *(cont')*
Meeting positive, action-oriented individuals	Managing details
Creating new products	Allowing others to have control over my life
Working out of my home	Commuting to work
Having big goals	Handling accounting/ bookkeeping

STRENGTHS	NEEDS IMPROVEMENT
Visionary/think big	Lacking financial resources
Action-oriented—accept total responsibility for my destiny	Limited network outside telecommunications industry
Passionate/enthusiastic/ energetic	Limited accounting/ finance knowledge
Successful sales background	Lacking balance in some areas of life
Extremely outgoing	Very hard on myself—perfectionist
Focused/committed	Aggressive—may come on too strong because of my enthusiasm
Resourceful and creative—think "out of the box"	Not tolerant of mediocrity
Believe in myself	Very fast paced, could easily run someone over if not careful

STRENGTHS(cont')	NEEDS IMPROVEMENT(cont')
Supported by family	Opinionated
Strong desire to be successful	Impatient

Action 2: Identify activities based on your loves. Based on your strengths and personal likes, identify three activities or goals you could set that are in line with your purpose. As an example, my purpose is to encourage others to become aware of the greater possibilities for their own lives and to take action. One could achieve that goal in an unlimited number of ways. For example, one could:

- Become a nun or a minister
- Join the Peace Corps
- Become a trainer inside a major corporation
- Teach an adult or child to read
- Donate time to a favorite charity
- Become a foster parent or grandparent
- Become a mentor
- Become a teacher
- Spearhead support groups at a church or synagogue
- Volunteer at a hospital
- Become a counselor on a hot line
- Spend time with a niece or nephew who needs support
- Write a book

By assessing my natural strengths, likes, and dislikes, it became clear to me, and probably to you too after reviewing my list, the activities that would not suit me. Becoming a nun, a trainer inside a major corporation, or joining the Peace Corps would not be top on my list. However, donating time to a charity, becoming a mentor, or writing a book would. Once I went through the process, my decision was easy.

Imagine how much richer your life could be if you injected passion into your life and career on a day-to-day basis. When you choose goals and activities that align with your purpose and support your natural strengths and loves, passion will automatically follow. You'll begin to view each day through wide-open eyes filled with expectation, wonder, and joy.

Find what you love and give yourself to it completely. Once you have, nothing can stop you.

·unstoppable·

"Years wrinkle the skin, but to give up enthusiasm wrinkles the soul"

—Anonymous

Characteristic Three

BELIEF
Sustains the Journey

What drove the individuals in this chapter to pursue their goals and not quit when *everyone* said it was impossible? Belief. They believed steadfastly in their dreams, even when no one else did. Belief is a prerequisite to becoming unstoppable. With a believing state of mind, you can transform your purpose and goals into physical realities. Once you truly believe and understand the power of belief, you can withstand any setback and adjust to every necessary change.

When belief develops into a conviction, when it is anchored in your soul and nothing can destroy it, then belief becomes faith. And faith is a powerful force.

The good news is you don't have to have faith the size of Texas to become unstoppable. A kernel of faith as small as a mustard seed is all that's required. After the stories, "Your Personal Action Plan" will provide a step-by-step process so you can develop your own unstoppable belief system.

In doing so, you'll leave the critics and obstacles behind and there will be no limits to what you can achieve.

■ **"I tell you the truth, if you have faith as small as a mustard seed, you can say to this mountain, 'Move from here to there' and it will move. Nothing will be impossible for you."**

—Matthew 17:20

■ UNSTOPPABLE ■

Road Warriors of a Different Kind

The Father, the Son, and the Fighting Spirit

It's impossible. A quadriplegic in a wheelchair, competing in marathons, triathlons, and even in the famously grueling Ironman race. It's impossible, and yet here he comes again, across the finish line, ahead of half the others in the race, with that radiant smile spectators have come to expect and love.

Rick Hoyt has crossed over 631 of those finish lines in the last twenty years, often in the top fifty percent, sometimes even as the winner. But he never crosses alone. Sometimes in front of him, sometimes behind, is the other half of the Hoyt team, his father, Dick.

People say what Dick does is impossible too—a middle-aged man jogging mile after mile, pushing another man in a wheelchair. Peddling Rick on a bicycle up and down unforgiving hills. Pulling Rick two miles or more through the water as he swims.

But the Hoyt family has made a habit of doing the impossible.

When Rick was born in 1962, the doctors told his parents, Dick and Judy, that their newborn son would bring them nothing but heartache and urged them to put him in an institution. As a spastic quadriplegic with cerebral palsy, Rick would live out his life as a vegetable. That's what the doctors said. Never, the doctors warned, could their son be mainstreamed into society.

The Hoyts ignored the experts' advice and brought their son to their home in North Reading, Massachusetts. Dick and Judy were determined to raise him just like they would any other child. Back then, experts didn't know a lot about cerebral palsy and weren't sure of the full extent of Rick's "disability." Learning to live with a child with severe disabilities was considered beyond the capabilities of almost any parent. But the Hoyts weren't typical parents. They set out to prove that "disabilities" are merely challenges meant to be overcome, not impassable barriers.

Rick's only way to communicate was by nodding his head yes or shaking it no. Speech professionals said he would never be able to speak. The Hoyts believed otherwise and raised $5,000 that they donated to Tufts University to help build the first interactive communicator. The device allowed a speechless person to "talk" by scrolling electronically through rows of letters and numbers and making selections to form complete messages. When Rick was twelve, the communicator was finally ready for testing. The engineers from Tufts and the entire Hoyt family excitedly stood around Rick, waiting for his first words. Rick used his head to touch an electronic switch, spelling out "Go Bruins!"

"We all laughed," said Dick, "because he confirmed what we had believed all along—Rick had a healthy, active mind—and a sense of humor."

Because of Rick's revealed interest in sports, the entire family took him fishing, canoeing, and even rock climbing, strapping him to his father's back. The family witnessed Rick's sense of adventure and challenge and saw a person with a normal mind, human needs, and hopes who longed to be respected. The interactive communicator played a key role in enabling Rick to express himself and his interests and revealed his curious, intelligent personality. Yet schools refused to enroll Rick since he could not walk, feed himself, or talk on his own. At fourteen, because of his increasing ability to "speak" through his communicator and a new law mandating the right of all children to attend school, Rick finally gained admittance to high school, where special aides helped him with physical tasks he was unable to handle himself. It was during this remarkable period of personal growth that Rick found the catalyst for his incredible athletic career.

In 1977, when Rick was sixteen, he learned of a five-mile road race that would be held to benefit a college student who was injured in an automobile accident. Using his communicator, Rick told his dad that he wanted to "run" in the race as his contribution. Dick's initial reaction was shock. "I thought, I'm forty, a guy who jogs a couple of days a week to keep my weight down, but hardly a seasoned runner. I was concerned about how I could participate in such a race pushing Rick in his wheelchair. But I knew it meant a lot to him so I said, 'Okay we'll try it.'"

After the race, Dick could hardly move for two weeks. He was in agony. But one night as he soaked his aching muscles in Epsom salts, Rick came home and typed a message that changed Dick's life forever: "Dad, when I'm running, it feels like I'm not handicapped anymore." Finally Rick had found something that gave him freedom like nothing else. At that point, Dick knew what he had to do. If Rick wanted to become an athlete and compete, Dick would loan him his arms and legs to make it happen. But to do so, Dick needed to design a lighter running chair so he wouldn't kill himself in the process.

Over the next two years, while Dick and an engineer designed and built the special chair, Rick and his father continued training and racing locally using the old chair. When the new chair was ready in September 1979, father and son entered their first official race, a five-mile race in Springfield, Massachusetts. They finished 150th out of 300 runners. They ran races in different cities every weekend. One of those races was the world-famous Boston Marathon—a grueling 26.2 miles. Rick and his father applied in the wheelchair division, where paraplegics had been racing on their own for years. But Rick, a quadriplegic who required a racing partner, was turned down. The Hoyts joined the race anyway, lining up behind the wheelchairs. Neither the sponsors nor the organizing committee would acknowledge their presence, but the spectators along the city streets did and they applauded and cheered them on. When the Hoyts finished, the crowd was jubilant. Out of 7,400 runners, the Hoyts finished in the top 90 percent; this race was the first of many Boston Marathons they would enter and finish.

During these years, Rick also proved himself to be much more than just an unusual athlete. He earned a degree in special education from Boston University, becoming the first "nonspeaking" quadriplegic to graduate from college.

By 1984, Dick had become an accomplished runner and was invited to race in triathlons. Triathlons are the Herculean races that combine long-distance swimming, long-distance bicycling, and cross-country running. The organizers wanted Dick—but only if he would compete alone. He refused. The next year the organizers made the same offer, but again Dick refused to participate without his son. Dick told the organizers, "Rick was the one that got me into this; I have no desire to compete alone. He is the one that drives me. Besides, without Rick, I wouldn't even know what to do with my arms."

Finally, the race officials approved Rick's participation if Dick could devise safe, durable equipment that would enable both of them to compete. Never mind that Dick didn't even know how to swim and hadn't been on a bicycle since he was six years old. After what his son had already accomplished, those seemed like small details to overcome.

Dick started training and devising the equipment that would help him tow Rick through water and pedal him by bicycle. The bicycle weighed 60 pounds, Rick weighed 90, and Dick weighed 170—that would be 320 pounds moving up and down hills, pushing relentlessly across agonizing physical and mental barriers. Rick and Dick completed that triathlon and every subsequent triathlon they entered, usually finishing in the top half of the competition.

Along the way, Dick developed a motto: "There is nothing we cannot do together." Dick was right. Together, father and son completed the infamous Ironman competition, a race most people are happy just to survive—2.4 miles of swimming, 112 miles on a bike, and 26.2 miles of running. Because of the extreme conditions of the Ironman race located on the big island of Hawaii—100-degree heat, high humidity, and unrelenting hills—this race required special preparation. To train, they competed in local races every weekend for a year. During the week while Rick was in school, Dick trained alone daily. He swam up to two miles, ran eight miles and biked thirty-five to forty miles while pushing a 100-pound bag of cement in Rick's running and biking chairs. Dick and his son have since competed in and finished four Ironman competitions.

They have also biked and run across the United States, from Los Angeles to Boston, covering 3,735 miles in forty-five days, without a single day off. And after completing fifteen Boston marathons—the race where they were initially rejected back in

1981—they were honored on the marathon's 100th anniversary as the event's centennial heroes.

Dick still insists it's his son, not him, who is the athlete. "I don't know what it is, but when I get behind his chair, there's something that happens. Rick is the driving force of the team. I loan him my body, but it's Rick's spirit that keeps us going."

Rick and Dick Hoyt have been competing for twenty years and say there's no end in site. What place they finish is not all that important. From the moment they took the starting line, every race has been a victory.

■ **"For as long as I can remember, people said I would never be able to do anything. My parents and I believed I could, and we've been proving them wrong ever since."**

—Rick Hoyt

·unstoppable·

"I claim to be no more
than an average man
with below average capabilities.
I have not the shadow of a doubt
that any man or woman
can achieve what I have
if he or she would put forth
the same effort and cultivate
the same hope and faith."

—Mahatma Gandhi

UNSTOPPABLE

What You Don't Know Won't Hurt You

In Fact, It Can Save Your Life!

Pam Lontos was uninformed and inexperienced and had about as much business savvy as a young schoolgirl. No wonder she's a success story.

She asked for jobs she had no right to ask for. She set unrealistic goals and then pursued them in unconventional ways. Over and over she placed her bets where the odds were the worst. She simply didn't know any better.

She didn't know any better because for much of her life she was controlled by other people. Growing up, her parents warned her against taking any kind of risks. She couldn't go to the beach because "she might drown"; she couldn't shop downtown with her friends because it was "too dangerous." When she married, her husband convinced her to give up studying psychology, the college major she loved, to study teaching, a profession that was more secure, but in which she had no interest.

After three unfulfilled years, Pam quit teaching and hoped that being a full-time mother and homemaker would bring meaning to her life. Instead, something else took control—her own despair.

It has happened to millions of women. Pam Lontos, with two children, a nice house in the suburbs, and a successful but emotionally distant husband, felt empty and useless. She was merely surviving and felt she was making no contribution. The more she realized it, the more depressed she became.

People deal with depression in different ways. Some take medication. Others resort to alcohol or drugs. Pam simply went to bed—and spent most of the next five years there. She rose every morning, took the kids to school, then went back to the blissful oblivion of sleep.

By the time Pam was in her thirties, she was sleeping eighteen hours a day and was forty pounds overweight. Her self-respect, confidence, and reason for living were completely gone. In her few hours of wakefulness, she contemplated suicide but could never actually do it. Her depression got so bad she was left with only one option.

If life was unlivable and if she couldn't kill herself, then the only choice was to change. "I spent my entire life waiting for someone else to do it for me, and no knight on a white horse had miraculously appeared." As daunting a task as change might seem, Pam was committed to crawling out of the black hole she had created to find a meaningful life.

Pam's first step back to the world was to join a health club in hopes of getting her body back in shape. It seemed like a small step, but the moment she walked through the doors of the health club, she walked into a new life.

Jim, the owner of the club, was an energetic, positive individual who sensed that Pam needed support. He encouraged her, promising she would see results if she stuck with it. He also lent her motivational tapes for inspiration. Pam listened to the tapes dozens of times.

As the pounds slowly dropped, so did Pam's fears. After several months, Pam had become brave enough to ask herself the one question she had never dared to ask: *What do I want to do?* As a teenager, she had sold shoes to help her family. Perhaps a career in sales would be something she'd enjoy. And since she experienced great results at the health club and really believed in it, she thought, why not start at the club?

Although she had no experience or training in membership sales, she asked Jim for a job selling club memberships. "You're the guy who gave me the tapes and got me motivated to do something with my life," she challenged him, "now you have to hire me!" He gave her the job, but that wasn't all. Jim also shared his optimistic philosophy about life and prodded Pam to overcome her fears. When Pam said she'd never driven downtown before and was afraid, Jim put her in the car, sat in the passenger's seat, gave her directions, and made her drive downtown.

As her confidence grew, so did her sales. Within weeks, Pam was driving all over town, outselling all the other salespeople. In a surprisingly short period, she'd come a long way. Jim's philosophy became her foundation: "Don't say you can't do something until you've tried!"

Pam's success that year prepared her for a new challenge. A new radio station opened in town. She convinced the general manager to hire her to sell advertising air time with the understanding she would receive no salary and work entirely on commission.

She didn't know that new stations are the toughest to sell since they have no established listening audience. She didn't know she was supposed to sell only to small companies because larger companies demanded bigger audiences. Because she didn't know, she boldly called on companies large and small and sold them based on the quality and buying power of the station's listening audience, rather than on the number of listeners.

Pam also didn't know that post-holiday January is always a bad sales month. So she put as much effort into January as she did into any other month, while the other salespeople slacked off, waiting for February. She earned one of the largest January commission checks ever written for radio sales in Dallas. From that point on, Pam was consistently the top revenue producer, selling as much as six other salespeople combined.

Pam's confidence grew and gave her the strength to confront her marital problems. After several attempts to work things out, she and her husband parted.

Life at the station also had its ups and downs, literally. The station's ratings dropped almost to the bottom of the market. But Pam didn't know it was customary in the business to bail out in rocky times. While everyone around her was quitting, she asked for the now vacant position of sales manager. Her boss, too stunned to argue, agreed. She had just taken the worst job possible and was actually excited about it!

At her first sales meeting, Pam wrote her projection for that month on the board: $100,000. Mouths fell open. Pam had been averaging $35,000 in sales every month. She thought the other three salespeople could do about the same. The general manager called her into his office after the meeting and explained that the station had only been averaging $42,000 per month—her $35,000 plus $7,000 from the other three salespeople combined. To set a goal of $100,000, he told her, was completely unrealistic.

That evening, Pam considered dropping the goal to $50,000. But on her way to work the next morning, she listened again to one of her favorite motivational tapes. She committed to hold strong to her "unrealistic" goal of $100,000. When she met with her team that morning, she restated her belief that they could do it.

By 4:30 P.M. on the last day of the month, sales for her team totaled $100,018. By December, sales had climbed to $140,000. Three months later, the figure was $180,000. The following November, Pam's sales team set a record of $272,000. These unprecedented results occurred despite the fact the station's listening audience grew only marginally.

After only two years of working at the station as a sales manager, Pam was promoted to vice president of sales, leapfrogging over the next logical position, which would have been general manager. She didn't know that it normally takes a minimum of five to ten years to reach that position and no one is ever promoted to vice president directly from a sales manager's position. "I'm glad I didn't know," said Pam, "or I might still be a sales manager."

After four successful years at the radio station, Pam left to start something new. Today Pam Lontos is a well-known motivational speaker, author, and sales and marketing consultant who is inspiring others to do exactly what she did—believe in possibilities, not limitations.

She has adopted a slogan that she uses whenever someone tells her a goal is impossible and she offers it to you:

> ■ **"You look them straight in the eye and say, 'Don't tell me it's impossible until after I've already done it.'"**
>
> *—Pam Lontos*

UNSTOPPABLE

"These motivational tapes have really inspired me! I'm going to make a million dollars, buy my own company and retire early. Then I'm going to write a novel and a symphony and give all the profits to charity. Then next month, I'll figure out how to do it!"

▪ Something to Think About ▪

Mark Sheppard, president of Texas Instruments, explained his triumph in the 1970s over industry giants like Westinghouse, GE, and RCA. "Those companies knew all the things that weren't possible," he said. "We didn't. We were stupid."

■ UNSTOPPABLE ■

From Zero to $15 Million

She Believed in Herself— Not the Experts

When Maria Elena Ibanez was a teenager in Colombia, her father enrolled her in a course on programming minicomputers.

Computers were becoming more common in Latin America, despite their $100,000 price tag, and Maria Elena was instantly taken with this revolutionary technology. In 1973, she went to the United States to study computer science at the college level. After graduation, she had an idea.

Personal computers were selling in the United States for $8,000—a fraction of what Latin American businesses were paying for their minicomputers. *Why not set up distribution of personal computers south of the border,* she thought, *where a fertile market was just waiting to be tapped?* She took her idea to the major computer companies in 1980 and asked for a chance to distribute their products in her home country.

"They told me to forget it," Maria Elena recalled. "The computer executives said Latin America was in the midst of an economic crisis. Latin America countries are poor, they don't have money. The executives considered it too small a market for them to pursue."

Maria Elena saw the situation differently. She perceived opportunity where others saw limitations. "I figured, even if the market was only $10 million, it was still big enough for me. I could make money in it. And nobody else would go after it because it was too small."

She was twenty-three years old, a woman, and had no sales or marketing experience, things the executives she encountered saw as three strikes against her. But she knew two things: computers were cheap in the United States, and Latin America needed them. Hopeful and optimistic, she approached a banker and requested a line of credit. He wanted to see her business plan. Maria Elena had never heard of such a thing. The second banker she approached asked for her marketing plan. She didn't know what that was, either. Then she tried to go directly to the distributors. Most wouldn't meet with her, but two listened skeptically. She asked, "How much business are you currently doing in Latin America?" They responded, "None." Maria Elena said, "I will sell $10,000 of your product a year in Latin America." Maria had to agree that all her orders would be prepaid. Altos Computers—with nothing to lose—gave her an exclusive distribution agreement for nine months.

Her next step was to call a travel agent. Maria Elena's instructions were simple: "Book me on a flight from Miami to Argentina, stopping in every major city I can without having to pay extra." That was how Maria Elena designed her marketing plan. She added, "Ignorance can be bliss and sometimes it pays off. I didn't know what I was getting myself into."

With no experience, belief in her goal and common sense became her guides. She landed in Colombia, checked into a hotel, opened the Yellow Pages, and began calling computer dealers. "I figured, the bigger the ad, the bigger the company. So I chose the companies that had the biggest ads first."

The next day, fully scheduled with appointments, she hit the pavement running. In the 1980s a woman engineer was rare and many Latin American businessmen were not used to dealing with women—particularly a petite, young blonde who looked about eighteen. She turned what might have been a disadvantage into an advantage by balancing her youthful enthusiasm with education and expertise. Maria Elena described her prospective customers' reaction to her: "They were fascinated by a young woman talking about the latest technology, things they didn't know. They responded very favorably because I had a tremendous product, the price was fantastic, and it allowed them to compete with the big guys."

A whirlwind three-week trip through Equador, Chile, Peru, and Argentina followed. In each country, she used the same Yellow Pages approach to market her product. "I had projected sales of $10,000 a year and returned to the United States, only three weeks later, with $100,000 worth of orders—prepaid—with cashier's checks in hand." For someone who earned $6 an hour tutoring at the university computer lab, the checks seemed like millions.

Eventually, Maria Elena's sales would be millions—many millions. In the next five years, Maria Elena's sales grew to an astounding $15 million. In 1987, *Inc.* magazine ranked her company, International Micro Systems, number 55 on its list of the 500 fastest-growing businesses. In 1988, Maria Elena sold the company and stayed on for another three years until sales reached $70 million.

Maria Elena has since started a new company selling computers to Africa. Once again, the marketing experts told her Africa was too poor for personal computer products, especially if they were sold by a non African female in a male-dominated culture. By now accustomed to negative responses, Maria Elena felt the experts were shortsighted. She believed in her own vision of the future. In 1991, she flew to Nairobi, the capital of Kenya, armed only with a catalog of products and a map. She checked into a hotel and picked up the Yellow Pages. Two weeks later, she flew home with $150,000 in orders.

Working first out of her garage, then out of a small warehouse, she began shipping products. More orders came in. In four months, she shipped $700,000 worth of computers. In her second year sales totaled $2.4 million, a figure that doubled the following year, and again the next. With sales averaging $13 million each year through the early 1990s, International High Tech Marketing made *Inc.'s* list of the 500 fastest-growing businesses. Maria Elena is the only person in the magazine's history to make the prestigious list with two separate companies built from zero capital.

Maria Elena Ibanez had good products to sell. But her success was built upon belief in herself and determination. There isn't a marketing plan in the world that can give you those.

■ "Everybody is an expert in giving advice on how you cannot do something. So forget about everybody. And then, when you encounter a hurdle—and I do that every week—view it as an opportunity, not the end of the world. Do whatever you need to do to get past it quickly. If you believe in your dream, you'll definitely get there."

—Maria Elena Ibanez

If you want to find some experts, start to do something. In 10 minutes, people will come from all around the world to tell you it can't be done.

▪ Something to Think About ▪

"We are our worst enemies since we 'know' what our limitations are. These female visionaries were capable of ignoring their own internal self-talk and functioned on a higher plane of optimistic euphoria. They did not know their limitations and therefore had none.

- Margaret Mead didn't know that a twenty-five-year-old unaccompanied female should not be wandering alone around the jungles of New Guinea and Samoa.
- Margaret Thatcher did not bother to ask whether a female prime minister of Great Britain was acceptable to her constituency.
- Oprah Winfrey was not deterred that Phil Donahue owned the daytime talk show market.

"They never asked the question and therefore moved into their castles in the sky as if it was their right to do so."

Excerpted from Gene Landrum's *Profiles of Female Genius*

▪ In Their Own Words ▪

"I was a mathematics graduate student *at the University of California, Berkeley. Arriving late to class as usual, I quickly copied the two math problems from the blackboard, assuming they were the homework assignment. When I sat down to work on them that evening, I found them to be the most difficult problems my professor had ever assigned. Night after night I worked, trying first to solve one then the other with no success. But I kept at it.*

"Several days later, I made a breakthrough and solved both problems. I took the homework to class the next day. The professor told me to leave it on his desk. It was piled so high with papers that I was concerned my homework would get lost in the clutter. Reluctantly, I dropped it off and went on my way.

"Six weeks later, on a Sunday morning, I was awakened by a pounding on the door. I was startled to see it was my professor. 'George! George!' he was shouting, 'You solved them!'

" 'Yes, of course,' I said. 'Wasn't I supposed to?' The professor explained that the two problems on the blackboard were not homework; they were two famous outstanding problems that leading mathematicians so far had not been able to solve. He could hardly believe that in only a few days I had solved them both.

"If someone had told me that they were two famous unsolved problems, I probably wouldn't have even tried to solve them. It goes to show the power of positive thinking."

George B. Dantzig

George Dantzig is a professor of Operations Research and Computer Science at Stanford University.

▪ Something to Think About ▪

A person has better odds of winning the lottery than making a National Basketball Association team. Now add to the equation being 5' 3" a full 16" shorter than the average NBA player. No one took Tyrone Bogues's life-long dream of becoming a professional basketball player serious except Tyrone. And that's why he became the smallest player in the history of the NBA.

■ "You can do anything you want to do in life, if you have a fierce belief in yourself, a strong will, a big heart, and some role models to inspire you."

—*Tyrone "Mugsy" Bogues,* In the Land of Giants

▪ In Their Own Words ▪

"For me to write, I had to quit *my job, live off my savings, and hope that what I was writing was not a pile of garbage but a salable manuscript. I had worked as a marketing consultant for eleven years and had become the first woman partner. Although I had a successful career, something was missing. The painful divorce I was going through caused me to reevaluate my life. As I thought about what I really wanted to do, a tiny inner voice said, 'You've always loved reading.' That's all it said. I was afraid to admit to myself that I wanted to write. Another voice asked, 'Who do you think you are?'*

"There was no reason for me to believe I could be a successful writer. I had always loved to read books but never had taken a course on writing. Yet, deep inside, I had always felt a need to tell stories. Up until that point, it was a dream I had never allowed myself to consider. Now, at thirty-five, I was whispering that dream to myself. But with that whisper came constant thoughts of negativity and self-doubt.

"Despite my fear, I quit my job and began to write. I committed to writing five pages a day, no matter what. If they stunk, they'd be five lousy pages, and if they were good, they'd be five good pages. Usually they were lousy.

"After two and a half years, I finally finished the hand-written manuscript and dropped it off to be professionally typed. It took me three months to muster the courage to pick it up. My inner voice was telling me, 'No one will ever buy it!' and I knew that once I picked it up the hardest part lay ahead—trying to sell it.

"I sent The First Wives Club *to eleven publishers and all I received were form letters stating, 'We don't read unsolicited*

manuscripts.' When I finally got an editor to read it, I received a rejection letter telling me the story was 'too unbelievable' and 'no one is interested in reading about middle-aged women who get dumped by their husbands.' I believed differently. Every bit of what happened to the women in my novel happened to me, my sister, my girlfriends, and women in my mother's generation. I knew there was a market for this type of book.

"So I started calling agents. After months, I found one to represent me. The first thing he insisted I do was change the manuscript. He believed that the women characters weren't sympathetic enough and recommended three changes: give the first wife a cat with leukemia, the second wife a mentally disabled daughter, and the third wife a baby that died. I was adamantly opposed to these changes. I didn't want the women to be unrealistically saintly or the husbands to be absolutely vile. Yet I reluctantly made the changes after many arguments, reasoning my agent was the 'expert' and knew what was best.

"Believe it or not, the expert's version was rejected at the publishing house where he had his best contacts. I was very depressed at that point. But by luck, the unpublished manuscript had gone out to Hollywood where Todd Harris found it and believed in it. He sent it to three women producers. Sherry Lansing, the CEO of Paramount Pictures, heard about my manuscript. She bought the rights and told me she liked everything about The First Wives Club *except three things: the cat with leukemia, the mentally disabled child, and the baby that died. I was amazed. I rewrote the book as closely as I could to my original and it was published by Simon and Schuster.*

"My experience taught me a lesson that I'll never forget: As long as you believe in yourself and your own vision, you have something. When you give up that, you are personally bankrupt."

Olivia Goldsmith is the author of the best-selling novel *The First Wives Club*, which later became a major motion picture and one of the biggest box office hits of 1996. She also has authored *Bestseller*, *Marrying Mom*, and *Switcheroo*.

"We're still pretty far apart. I'm looking for a six-figure advance and they're refusing to read the manuscript."

▪ Something to Think About ▪

Mary Kay Ash's mascot for her cosmetics company is a bumblebee. "Because of its tiny wings and heavy body, aerodynamically the bumblebee shouldn't be able to fly. But the bumblebee doesn't know that, so it flies anyway."

▪ In Their Own Words ▪

"I was caught in a dilemma. *On one hand, I wanted badly to become a nurse. The idea of helping people really appealed to me. On the other hand, studying four hours a day had no appeal. My grades showed it. At the age of nineteen, I failed my first year of nursing school. The next year I failed again.*

"In the nursing program, there was a teacher I will never forget. She had little patience for anyone who wasn't totally committed to the program, and my half-hearted efforts sadly put me in that category. Bluntly, she told me that I didn't have what it took to become a nurse and that I should drop out!

"Her words played continuously in my mind. Maybe I wasn't good enough. After my second failed attempt, I was sure I wasn't good enough. Humiliated by my failure, I moved to another city, away from my family and friends. I needed time to sort out my life. I had to find some sort of job, and because I loved the hospital environment, I took a position as a medical transcriptionist. The job went well, but I couldn't get nursing out of my mind. It became clear that I wouldn't be satisfied doing anything else. But my desire to become a nurse was threatened by an equally compelling fear of failure.

"Every year for five years, I planned to go back to school. And every year I was paralyzed by the fear of failing again. When it was time to enroll, I found endless excuses for not signing up. I was too busy. I couldn't afford it. I was needed at my job.

"Years passed and I was no closer to what I really wanted. Realizing I didn't have the strength within me to do it alone, I asked God for help. I asked Him to grant me the ability to achieve my goal. I started reading the Bible, and friends recommended several books that introduced me to the concept of positive thinking. My faith grew, and with

it, my courage and self-esteem. Over time, I was strengthened by my belief that with God's help there was nothing I couldn't do.

"It was 1978. That year when enrollment opened for the nursing program, I walked through the door. Was I nervous? You bet! But I was also confident that He would get me through. Two years later, I graduated with honors in the top 5 percent of my class. Joyfully, I have been a nurse ever since.

"It took me five years to discover my faith, to build my confidence, and to find the courage to try one more time."

Suzan Robison

Suzan Robison works full time as a Registered Nurse in Orlando, Florida.

.unstoppable.

"I am the greatest.
I said that even before I knew I was.
Don't tell me I can't do something.
Don't tell me it's impossible.
Don't tell me I'm not the greatest.
I'm the double greatest."

—Muhammad Ali, Professional Boxer

Your Personal Action Plan

Charting Your Journey to Belief

You've identified your purpose and set goals that you're passionate about. Now you're ready to make it happen. Eagerly, you share your idea with a friend over morning coffee. Before you can get out two sentences, your friend cautions you that what you want to do has been tried before—unsuccessfully, mind you—and perhaps this isn't the right time for you to throw caution to the wind. After considering your friend's comments, you can't help but wonder, *Maybe this is going to be a little more difficult than I had planned.*

If you reach the end of the day without claiming temporary insanity for conceiving such a ridiculous idea in the first place, consider it a victory. Without a doubt, your dream is most vulnerable immediately after its inception.

The most important step you can take to keep your dream alive is to pursue activities that will strengthen your belief system and minimize your vulnerabilities. Just as our body's immune system can be bolstered by proper diet, exercise, and relaxation techniques, our belief system can be nurtured and strengthened as well. Fortunately, we can take specific actions to achieve this goal.

Ten Steps to Developing an Unstoppable Belief System

Step 1: Take Immediate Action

You might wonder what taking action has to do with strengthening your belief system. Your actions reflect your beliefs, and it is what you do that demonstrates what you believe. By taking even the smallest steps, you are communicating to yourself and to the world that you believe in yourself and your dream.

In the beginning, you may not *feel* very brave and confident, much less unstoppable. However, by taking consistent action, you will generate the feeling until eventually you are confident, down to the bottom of your soul. Every action you take raises your self-esteem and confidence. You're no longer sitting around waiting and hoping for something magical to happen. You're the creator of that "magic." With your growing self-esteem, you realize your dream is possible.

Mary Kay Ash, founder of the famous cosmetics company, advises her colleagues to "fake it until you make it." She knows a great secret: if people can see themselves as the person they hope to become and act "as if" they are that person, soon they will not be acting. They will actually become that person. If you want to be unstoppable, show the world that you believe in yourself. Act confident; act with conviction.

Action: Write down one action you can take immediately that will put your dream into motion. Do it now!

Step 2: Acknowledge Your Untapped Potential

It is commonly agreed that the average person uses only a fraction of his or her potential mental capacity. It is important to acknowledge that we don't use anywhere close to our fullest capabilities and that we have an enormous potential within us to do and be much more.

Action: Make a realistic assessment of your current abilities. Now imagine that your abilities have increased by 10 percent. What would you be doing if you immediately possessed 10 percent more abilities, skills, and talents. You could be doing those things today if you believed you could and pushed yourself—even a little bit—outside your comfort zone.

■ **"Everything is possible for him who believes."**

Mark 9:23

Step 3: Watch Your Internal Language!

Are you plagued by negative thoughts? The "yeah, buts?" It is critical that you cut those thoughts off as soon as they start. You may have heard the expression "thoughts are things." Whatever you think about constantly, you will achieve. If you're continually focusing on how difficult your goal is, you will never achieve it.

You can overcome negative thoughts by focusing on the possibilities. To illustrate the power of our words, think of a challenging goal and then say to yourself, *How on earth did I think I could ever accomplish my goal? It's too big, too difficult. It's impossible! What was I thinking?*

Sound familiar? Maybe you never have those types of inner conversations, but I've had to fight that internal dialog on more than one occasion! When those thoughts come to mind, immediately replace them with the following type of mental conversation: *I know my goal is achievable because others have accomplished it before me. I am absolutely committed to making it happen and am willing to do whatever is necessary to achieve my true heart's desire.*

Do you feel the difference in the two? If you dwell very long on the first conversation, you'll be in trouble. The second conversation, however, immediately renews your commitment and transports you to a new world of possibility. While in that positive state of mind, you are open to asking better questions. What can I do to achieve my goal? Who might be willing to help? How can I approach this differently and achieve my desired result?

> **Action:** List some of the negative self-talk in which you routinely engage. Think of how you could modify that dialog to have a positive effect on your thinking and on the results. For example, instead of asking yourself, *Why me?* or *Why can't I?* Ask yourself, *What can I do to make things better, to turn my life around, to improve the situation, to achieve what I long for?* These questions instantly change your focus and empower you.

■ **"I tried to block out all negative thoughts. I kept reading books on faith that tell you to just keep exercising your faith and continue to believe."**

—Jackie Joyner-Kersee

Step 4: Neutralize Fear and Risk

Fear is a natural reaction to change. It's probably the number one reason people hesitate to start anything new and opt instead for the way things are—safe, comfortable, and familiar. It's important to realize that *everyone* experiences fear when venturing into unknown territory. Fear is a natural and physiological response designed to alert us to the fact that we need to prepare to cope or we need to escape. However, the difference between successful and unsuccessful people is their response to fear. Successful people acknowledge fear and manage it by confronting the cause and determining how they can prepare for the challenge ahead. They decide on certain actions that will enable them to feel as competent and confident as possible.

My personal strategy for managing fear has always been to thoroughly prepare. Whether I'm giving an important sales presentation or speaking in front of a large audience, I never "wing it." Initially, the task may seem daunting, but the more prepared I am, the more confident I become.

Lilly Walters wrote in her book *Secrets of Successful Speakers*, "Rehearsal and preparation can reduce your fear by 75 percent." She continued, "Deep breathing will take care of an additional 15 percent. Ten percent will be conquered through mental preparation." Those are percentages that can make a huge difference in your mental state.

To overcome fear, we must plunge ourselves into the very thing we fear most. Only then, by taking risks, can we build our confidence. In a study conducted by Cornell University, senior citizens were asked if they had any regrets about their lives. The overwhelming response was that they most regretted not doing what they had always wanted to do. It was the risks they *didn't* take—not the risks they took—that haunted them.

Don't let fear create the same regrets for you. Acknowledge fear. Prepare for it. Then act.

Action: Identify one fear that is stopping you from achieving your goals. Neutralize it by deciding what you can do to prepare yourself for the challenge. Then make the commitment to do so. If the outcome isn't what you planned, congratulate yourself for your courage and consider what you've learned from the experience. Modify your plan and take action again. (In chapter 4, we will discuss a step-by-step process to create your own unstoppable plan.)

■ **"You are a child of God. Your playing small does not serve the world. There is nothing enlightening about shrinking, so that other people won't feel insecure around you. We are born to make manifest the glory of God that is within us. It is not just in some of us; it is in everyone. And as we let our light shine, we unconsciously give other people permission to do the same. As we are liberated from our own fear, our presence automatically liberates others."**

—Nelson Mandela

Step 5: Visualize Success

Robert Kennedy, quoting George Bernard Shaw, said "Some…see things as they are and ask *Why*. I see things as they could be and ask *Why not?*" His words became an anthem for a society weary of its limitations and anxious to rediscover its potential.

To visualize all that could be is not just to think about it but to actively see it. This process of imagination, when directed, is known as visualization. Visualizing what you want before it happens is one of the most powerful strategies of achievers, thousands of whom use visualization to rekindle their passions, clarify their goals, and strengthen their faith.

If you want to become a successful speaker, for example, first picture yourself in front of an audience. *See* yourself eloquently speaking to hundreds of attentive listeners. *Hear* the confidence and vitality in your voice and the encouraging words people offer you. *Feel* the warmth and receptivity of the audience. *Smell* the fragrance of flowers that have been placed on the stage. *Taste* the cool water that you sip from a glass.

To create such a clear, strong vision, you need only release your abundant imagination. In the same way, when you have developed a goal, visualize it with as much detail and imagery as you can, exactly as you want and expect it to happen. Make your vision so powerful that when you finally accomplish your goal, you have a sense of deja vu—"haven't I experienced this before?" Yes, you have—in your imagination a thousand times—and each time the experience became more and more real.

Martin Short practiced visualization regularly as an eight-year-old child. He fantasized about being an entertainer. In his attic, he would do *The Martin Short Show*. He sang, interviewed people, and played an applause record after each glowing performance. He even went so far as to type up who his show's guests would be for his *TV Guide* listing. His success as an entertainer confirms the power of visualization.

Action: Identify a specific goal that supports your purpose and passion. Imagine yourself achieving that goal in every detail. Think about where you are at that moment, what you are wearing, who is with you, what the temperature is, and what kind of feelings you're experiencing. Create the most compelling and exciting vision you can imagine. Then write down what you have visualized or record it on a cassette tape. To enhance the recording you could add background music or peaceful nature sounds.

Read your description or listen to your tape every single day. As you do, your belief and confidence will grow. And as your belief grows, you'll be able to take further actions. Before long, you'll be operating from a foundation of firm, unstoppable faith.

> ■ **"Success is a state of mind. If you want success, start seeing yourself as a success."**
>
> *—Dr. Joyce Brothers*

Step 6: Practice Affirmations

Napoleon Hill, author of the best-selling *Think and Grow Rich*, suggests that repeating positive affirmations to your subconscious mind is an excellent method for developing faith. After continually repeating an affirmation to oneself, eventually you come to believe it.

Action: Make a list or write a statement of exactly what you want to accomplish. Go to a quiet spot where you can close your eyes and repeat aloud your written statement. As you repeat your statement, envision yourself having accomplished your goal. Repeat your statement morning and night and you will find yourself getting closer and closer to your goal. Place a written copy of your goal where you can see it morning and night.

> ■ **"For as he thinketh in his heart, so is he."**
>
> *—Proverbs 23:7*

Step 7: Find Others to Believe with You

It's hard enough staying positive during challenging times even when you are supported by positive people. Associating with negative people can mean the certain death of your dream. Many of the people in this book had no time for people who were negative and nonsupportive. John Johnson, founder of *Ebony* magazine, (whom you'll meet in chapter 6) fired any employee who said his goals were unachievable. Billy Payne (whose story you'll find in chapter 5), organizer of the 1996 Olympics, steered clear of anyone, including experts and consultants, who said his dream could not be realized. You would do well to follow their lead.

Unfortunately, it may be difficult to eliminate all the negative people from your life. Your mother or father, a business associate, a best friend, or even your spouse might be a negative influence. And since many of these people have known you for years, they probably think of you in terms of your past experiences and not in terms of who you are today or the person you can become. For example, when you shared your dream of performing on Broadway, your brother couldn't get past the memory of seeing you fall off the stage during your first school play. Or when you told your mother you were starting a company that organizes closets, she nearly fainted, remembering your teenage years when she didn't dare *open* your closet door. The saying "A prophet has no honor in his own home" couldn't be more true.

Sometimes it's easier to find support from a complete stranger. A stranger doesn't carry preconceived ideas about what you can or cannot do. In chapter 6, we will discuss how you can meet supportive people to build your team. The message at this point is that everyone needs someone to believe in him or her, and those who are closest to you may not be the best people to fill that role. The key is to find someone who does.

Action: Take an inventory of the people in your life. Identify one or two individuals who are supportive and can provide encouragement. If you can't think of one person who fits into that category, chapter 6 identifies the best places to meet people who can. In the initial stages of implementing your dream, share it only with supportive people. As your dream takes shape and you become stronger in your belief, you'll be able to handle the multitude of naysayers who will inevitably cross your path. In the beginning, however, be selective.

One of my researchers told me that I treat negativity "like poison," and she was right. Negativity works like poison in the bloodstream: if you give into its power, it will weaken your confidence and kill your dream. Your goals are simply too important to let that happen!

Step 8: Draw Strength from a Higher Power

So many of the unstoppable individuals we read about drew strength from God. By relying on Him, they were able to overcome profound obstacles and self-doubt. I have drawn strength from adopting two beliefs. The first is that God loves me. The second is that everything happens for a reason and ultimately that reason will serve me. When you develop a belief that in every adversity there is the seed of an equal or greater benefit, you cannot help but learn from the experience and be hopeful about the future.

Action: In his book *The Power of Positive Thinking*, Dr. Norman Vincent Peale suggests we repeat many times daily, "God is with me; God is helping me; God is guiding me."

Acknowledge that God is with you and nothing can defeat you. Believe that you receive power from your Creator. By stating an affirmation such as this several times each day and visualizing God's presence, your faith will deepen.

■ **"My faith means a lot to me. I don't feel that I have to do it all on my own. I think I can face challenging situations and feel there's a source of strength beyond myself, that it's not all just on my shoulders."**

—Elizabeth Dole

.unstoppable.

"Often your tasks will be many,
And more than you think you can do...
Often the road will be rugged
And the hills insurmountable, too...

But always remember, the hills ahead
Are never as steep as they seem,
And with faith in your heart start upward
And climb 'til you reach your dream,

For nothing in life that is worthy
Is ever too hard to achieve
If you have the faith to try it
And you have the faith to believe...

For faith is a force that is greater
Than knowledge or power or skill
And many defeats turn to triumph
If you trust in god's wisdom and will...

For faith is a mover of mountains,
There's nothing that god cannot do,
So start out today with faith in your heart
And 'climb 'til your dream comes true!'"

—Helen Steiner Rice

CLIMB 'TIL YOUR DREAM COMES TRUE

Step 9: Dealing with Critics and Rejection

> ■ **"I am looking for a lot of men who have an infinite capacity to not know what can't be done."**
>
> *—Henry Ford*

They say that "everybody's a critic," and that never seems more true than when you're pursuing a dream and trying to enlist support. There will always be well-meaning people who want to "protect" you from your "unrealistic fantasies." Critics tried to discourage many of the people you are reading about in this book. Critics said these people were unqualified; their ideas wouldn't work; there was no market for their products; they were too short, too young, too early, or too late. And all of the people in this book ignored the negative input and achieved their goals.

The only opinion about your dream that really counts is yours. The negative comments of others merely reflect *their* limitations—*not yours*. There is nothing unrealistic about a dream that aligns with your purpose, ignites your passion, and inspires you to plan and persevere until you attain it. On the contrary, it is unrealistic to expect a person with such drive and commitment *not* to succeed.

Action: Do your homework. The most effective way to counter negativity is to learn all you can about what you want to accomplish. Identify the primary challenges you will face while pursuing your goal. Formulate strategies for overcoming each one. Armed with knowledge and a plan, you will be in a much stronger position and more confident when your critics offer unwanted advice.

When I told people I was not only going to write a book, but was committed to writing a best-selling book, I was told on more than one occasion that my goal was unrealistic and it was highly improbable that it would happen. I didn't accept their advice because I had done my homework. I had researched the publishing industry and developed a strategy based on what other best-selling authors and publishing companies had done. By following their examples, I believed I could also create a best-selling book. If they did it, so could I.

The following individuals came up against a few naysayers of their own. Fortunately, these individuals didn't listen.

Critics' Corner

- *"How long will you go on training all day in a gymnasium and living in a dream world?"*

  Arnold Schwarzenegger's family's pleas for him to get a "respectable" job, not understanding his desire to become Mr. Universe.

- *"Liquidate the business right now and recoup whatever cash you can. If you don't, you'll end up penniless."*

  The attorney of cosmetic tycoon Mary Kay Ash, weeks before she opened her first store.

- *"It's a cutthroat business and you've got no chance of success."*

  Accountant for Estee Lauder, founder of a multibillion dollar cosmetics empire.

- *"The language on the floor is too rough and there's no ladies' room."*

  The response of officials of the New York Stock Exchange

when Muriel Siebert wanted to buy a seat in 1967. She bought a seat on the exchange anyway and remained the only woman there for nine years.

- *"You have the perfect voice for broadcasting, but you should get a job as a secretary. We're not using women."*

  What announcers for NBC Radio told Sally Jessy Raphael when she applied for a job after graduation from Columbia University.

- *"Working out with weights causes athletes to lose their speed and agility. Bodybuilding causes hemorrhoids and hernias."*

  The view of health experts who called future fitness guru and TV star Jack LaLanne "a nut."

- *"You can't play the piano, and God knows you can't sing. You'd better learn how to weave chairs so you can support yourself."*

  A comment by Ray Charles's teachers.

- *"It's too hard to crack into the late-night ratings. Television isn't ready for a black talk show host. This is America, and you can forget it."*

  Conventional "wisdom," prior to Arsenio Hall's acceptance of Paramount's offer to host a late-night talk show.

- *"You have a nice voice, but it's nothing special."*

  What a teacher said when rejecting Diana Ross after she auditioned for a part in a high school musical.

- *"You will never make the cover of Vogue because you don't have blond hair or blue eyes."*

  A remark to Cher by photographer Richard Avedon. When

Cher did appear on the cover, Vogue sold more copies than it had ever sold before.

- *"You're a good editor with a promising future in the business. Why would you want to throw it all away to try to be a writer? I read your book. Frankly, it's not really that good."*

  A New York publisher's comments to James Michener about his first book, *Tales of the South Pacific*, for which Michener won a Pulitzer Prize.

- *"You're foolish to try to sell sparkling water in the land of Coca-Cola drinkers."*

  Advice given to Gustave Leven by several consulting firms' when hearing about his plans to launch Perrier in the United States.

Step 10: Dealing with Experts

- **"In the beginner's mind there are many possibilities, in the expert's mind there are few."**

—Shunryu Suzuki, Scholar

Another type of critic, a little different from naysayers—and certainly more threatening—is the "expert." *Webster's* defines an expert as one who is "knowledgeable through training and experience." An expert can certainly be more intimidating than your Uncle Joe who knows nothing about your field but everything about what you should do in it.

Experts can offer insight and be a great resource. However, consider the following:

- Expert knowledge is based on past experience; it may not apply to an innovative idea for the future.
- Experts are seldom known for their creativity and imagination. Pioneers and innovators use their intuition; experts use data. That data may apply to past models and have no relevance whatsoever to present or future models. Peter Drucker, one of the most respected voices in the business world wrote, "market research does not work. One cannot do market research on something that does not exist." The dreamer's domain is that of the unproven and the possible, and that domain is alien territory for the expert.
- Experts have a vested interest in preserving the status quo. Gene Landrum offers this insight in his book, *Profiles of Genius*. "A major problem with expert opinion is the tendency of the expert to have a strong desire to preserve and validate the present way of things, since experts happen to have an ego investment in the very thing in which they are considered an expert. If they should invest in its destruction, they are in essence destroying some of their own credibility. Therefore the expert never capitulates. That is why Thomas Kuhn was able to show that it takes thirty years (*The Structure of Scientific Revolutions*, 1959) for any new concept to gain acceptance. Other research has shown that older scientists die (Wilson, 1990) before accepting new concepts that violate their own beliefs in reality."

Let's take a look at some actual expert opinions offered to visionary entrepreneurs of the not-so-distant past.

- *"No one will stand in front of a TV screen and play a game with no physical action, like pinball."*

  Executive's comments after viewing an early demonstration of Pong, the first video game by Atari founder Nolan Bushnell.

- *"No one will buy a tape player that doesn't record."*

  Opinion of market researchers at Sony when chairman Akio Morita first proposed the Walkman.

- *"It's a huge risk, and it will never fly."*

  Aeronautical engineer's evaluation of Bill Lear's design for a jet.

- *"Personal computers are a hobbyist fad."*

  Prediction of IBM, Intel, HP, Atari, and countless other electronics companies.

- *"People will rent videotapes, but they'll never buy them."*

  Opinion of media experts who were later proven wrong by Jane Fonda's exercise tapes.

- *"A global, twenty-four-hour news network will never work."*

  Network executives response to Ted Turner's plans for CNN.

- *"There's no market for it. If there were, major airlines would already be offering it. You won't be able to find reliable couriers."*

  Conclusion of advisors to Fred Smith, founder of Federal Express.

Action: The next time an "expert" attacks your dream, take comfort in realizing that people who achieved some of the greatest accomplishments of humankind were also told their goals were not possible. Trust your intuition and your inner heart's desire, and continue forward. Your confidence will grow every time you take a risk and overcome the fear of the unknown.

Being unstoppable has little to do with evaluations of experts, past experience, industry pedigrees, or IQs. Intellect and reason do not propel your dream forward; intuition, imagination, and faith do. The boldness of faith is so powerful that it will leave critics and experts astounded at your results.

Believe in yourself and there will come a day when others will have no choice but to believe with you.

·Characteristic Four·

PREPARATION Builds the Foundation

Planning was a vital component in the success of each of the individuals featured in this chapter. They planned, researched, sought advice, collected information, developed skills, and prepared themselves thoroughly for the fulfillment of their dreams. By the time opportunity arrived, they were ready.

The average individual has no real plan for his or her future. He or she may have fantasies and even hopes, but not plans. In "Your Personal Action Plan," we'll discuss how to develop a clear vision of what you want to accomplish and identify the steps to formulate an unstoppable plan for your life.

■ **"There is no sudden leap into the stratosphere. There is only advancing step by step, slowly and torturously, up the pyramid toward your goals."**

—Ben Stein

■ UNSTOPPABLE ■

A Lifetime of Planning Pays Off

To This Ex-Cop, Selling Burgers Meant Selling Hope

"You gotta be crazy!" That's what Lee Dunham's friends told him back in 1971 when he gave up a secure job as a police officer and invested his life savings in the notoriously risky restaurant business. This particular restaurant was more than just risky, it was downright dangerous. It was the first McDonald's franchise in the city of New York—smack in the middle of crime-ridden Harlem.

Lee had always had plans. When other kids were playing ball in the empty lots of Brooklyn, Lee was playing entrepreneur, collecting milk bottles and returning them to grocery stores for the deposits. He had his own shoeshine stand and worked delivering newspapers and groceries. Early on, he promised his mother that one day she would never again have to wash other people's clothes for a living. He was going to start his own business and support her. "Hush your mouth and do your homework," she told him. She knew that no member of the Dunham family had ever risen above the level of laborer, let alone owned a business. "There's no way you're going to open your own business," his mother told him repeatedly.

Years passed, but Lee's penchant for dreaming and planning did not. After high school, he joined the Air Force, where his goal of one day owning a family restaurant began to take shape. He enrolled in the Air Force food service school and became such an accomplished cook he was promoted to the officers' dining hall.

When he left the Air Force, he worked for four years in several restaurants, including one in the famed Waldorf Astoria Hotel in New York. Lee longed to start his own restaurant but felt he lacked the business skills to be successful. He signed up for business school and took classes at night while he applied and was hired to be a police officer.

For fifteen years he worked full-time as a police officer. In his off-hours, he worked part-time as a carpenter and continued to attend business school. "I saved every penny I earned as a police officer," he recalled. "For ten years, I didn't spend one dime—there were no movies, no vacations, no trips to the ballpark. There were only work and study and my lifelong dream of owning my own business." By 1971, Lee had saved $42,000, and it was time for him to make his vision a reality.

Lee wanted to open an upscale restaurant in Brooklyn. With a business plan in hand, he set out to seek financing. The banks refused him. Unable to get funding to open an independent restaurant, Lee turned to franchising and filled out numerous applications. McDonald's offered him a franchise, with one stipulation: Lee had to set up a McDonald's in the inner city, the first to be located there. McDonald's wanted to find out if its type of fast-food restaurant could be successful in the inner city. It seemed that Lee might be the right person to operate that first restaurant.

To get the franchise, Lee would have to invest his life savings and borrow $150,000 more. Everything for which he'd worked and sacrificed all those years would be on the line—a very thin line if he believed his friends. Lee spent many sleepless nights before making his decision. In the end, he put his faith in the years of preparation he'd invested—the dreaming, planning, studying and saving—and signed on the dotted line to operate the first inner-city McDonald's in the United States.

The first few months were a disaster. Gang fights, gunfire, and other violent incidents plagued his restaurant and scared customers away. Inside, employees stole his food and cash, and his safe was broken into routinely. To make matters worse, Lee couldn't get any help from McDonald's headquarters; the company's representatives were too afraid to venture into the ghetto. Lee was on his own.

Although he had been robbed of his merchandise, his profits, and his confidence, Lee was not going to be robbed of his dream. Lee fell back on what he had always believed in—preparation and planning.

Lee put together a strategy. First, he sent a strong message to the neighborhood thugs that McDonald's wasn't going to be their turf. To make his ultimatum stick, he needed to offer an alternative to crime and violence. In the eyes of those kids, Lee saw the same look of helplessness he had seen in his own family. He knew that there was hope and opportunity in that neighborhood and he was going to prove it to the kids. He decided to serve more than meals to his community—he would serve solutions.

Lee spoke openly with gang members, challenging them to rebuild their lives. Then he did what some might say was unthinkable: he hired gang members and put them to work. He tightened up his operation and conducted spot checks on cashiers to weed out thieves. Lee improved working conditions and once a week he offered his employees classes in customer service and management. He encouraged them to develop personal and professional goals. He always stressed two things: his restaurant offered a way out of a dead-end life and the faster and more efficiently the employees served the customers, the more lucrative that way would be.

In the community, Lee sponsored athletic teams and scholarships to get kids off the streets and into community centers and schools. The New York inner-city restaurant became McDonald's most profitable franchise worldwide, earning more than $1.5 million a year. Company representatives who wouldn't set foot in Harlem months earlier now flocked to Lee's doors, eager to learn how he did it. To Lee, the answer was simple: "Serve the customers, the employees, and the community."

Today, Lee Dunham owns nine restaurants, employs 435 people, and serves thousands of meals every day. It's been many years since his mother had to take in wash to pay the bills. More importantly, Lee paved the way for thousands of African-American entrepreneurs who are working to make their dreams a reality, helping their communities, and serving up hope.

All this was possible because a little boy understood the need to dream, to plan, and to prepare for the future. In doing so, he changed his life and the lives of others.

■ **"I've always had a vision to do bigger and better things. Not just for myself, but for my family and community. I know you don't do it all at once. It takes planning and preparation to get big things done, and I was willing to spend fifteen years preparing myself for the challenge."**

—Lee Dunham

.unstoppable.

"I don't know if anybody really skyrockets to success. I think that success is a process. And I believe that my first Easter speech, at Kosciusko Baptist Church at the age of three and a half, was the beginning. And that every other speech, every other book I read, every other time I spoke in public, was a building block. By the time I first sat down to audition in front of a television camera and somebody said, 'Read this,' what allowed me to read it so comfortably was the fact that I had been doing it a while...I think luck is preparation meeting opportunity."

—Oprah Winfrey

■ UNSTOPPABLE ■

Preparing to Win

How Maury Wills Got to First Base—and Kept Going

If there was ever an improbable prospect for major league baseball stardom, that longshot was Maury Wills. When he first tried out for the Brooklyn Dodgers in 1950, he stood five feet eight inches tall and weighed 150 pounds—too small to play most positions. He was a terrific sprinter, a promising pitcher, and a good fielder, but he couldn't hit worth a darn. The Dodgers signed him but sent him down to the minor leagues for development. Maury told his friends, "In two years, I'm going to be in Brooklyn playing with Jackie Robinson."

Despite that confidence, Maury languished in the minors for eight and a half frustrating years. How he finally got out—to reach not just the major leagues but individual greatness—is a story of patience, preparation, and practice, practice, practice.

He started out in Class D, the lowest rung on the baseball ladder, riding a bus from game to game, enduring racial harassment in segregated towns, and barely supporting his growing family on his paltry $150-a-month minor league salary. He knew he had something to offer a big league club if he could just round out his skills.

Every day, Maury practiced hitting for hours. Yet after years of grueling practice and drills, he was still far short of making a major league roster. Instead of giving up, he changed his game. During practice one day, the team manager, Bobby Bragan, watched as Maury took a couple of swings at the plate from the left side. Bobby knew Maury was afraid of getting hit in the head with a curve ball, and Bobby knew if a player couldn't hit a curve ball, he would never make the majors. Bobby suggested Maury try "switch-hitting"—learning to hit left-handed as well as right-handed so he would feel safer batting against right-handed pitchers from the opposite side of home plate.

"You're in a seven-and-a-half-year slump as a right-handed batter," Bobby told him. "You've got nothing to lose. Come out early tomorrow and I'll throw to you." The next morning, hours before the other players arrived, Bobby threw to Maury and saw new promise. After four days, Maury was eager to try switch-hitting, but Bobby suggested he wait until the team went on a road trip so Maury wouldn't embarrass himself in front of the home fans. Two weeks later, that opportunity finally came.

Maury got two hits. "I began to feel like a baseball player again," said Maury. "Those two hits restored my hope and vision of going to Brooklyn." By the end of the season, Maury had polished his skills at shortstop and showed promise as a switch-hitter. Even with his improved skills, the Brooklyn Dodgers still did not offer to move him up.

In his eighth year in the minors, Maury continued to practice with Bobby. In the first twenty-five games he stole twenty-five bases and hit .313. Meanwhile, the Dodgers' shortstop broke his toe and the general manager was looking nationwide for a replacement. Bobby Bragan called the home office. "You're looking around the country for a shortstop and you've got one right here," he said. "Maury Wills?" was their response. "He can't play. He's been around forever."

"Yeah," Bobby said. "But he's a different player now."

The Dodgers ignored Bobby's advice and continued the search. A week later, out of desperation, the home office called Maury, and he flew to join the team in Milwaukee. In the next couple of games, Maury came to a painful realization—playing in the major leagues was much different from playing in the minors. Although Maury was a fine shortstop, his hitting *still* wasn't major league caliber. The managers let him bat a couple of times each game then took him out around the seventh inning and put in a pinch hitter. "The handwriting was on the wall and I knew if I didn't learn to hit better, I was going back to the minors," Maury remembered.

But now that Maury had finally tasted his dream, he wasn't about to go back to the minors.

Maury went to the first base coach, Pete Reiser, and asked for help. Pete agreed to meet Maury for batting practice two hours before the team's regular practice session each day. Maury practiced hitting day after day, in every kind of weather, until his hands were blistered and bleeding. Yet for all his efforts, his batting still wasn't strong enough. He continued to be taken out in the seventh inning. Discouraged, Maury finally considered quitting baseball.

Pete wouldn't let Maury quit. Pete realized that a crucial piece of Maury's preparation had been missing. All this time, Maury had been working on his hands, arms, posture, and swing through. Pete wondered if perhaps the biggest obstacle was Maury's confidence. So Pete changed the training. Each session, Pete and Maury spent thirty minutes hitting the ball and ninety minutes working on Maury's mental preparation. Sitting in the outfield, Pete would focus on Maury's thinking and attitude. Pete assured Maury that he had what it took and that if he persisted in his training, the work would eventually pay off.

"It was tough to continue to walk up to that plate having no hits in ten times at bat," Maury said. "However, I learned that confidence comes only after a measure of success, and success comes after a whole lot of practice and preparation."

In a game two weeks later, Maury got a hit his first time at bat. And his second time at bat. In the now-dreaded seventh inning, Maury looked over his shoulder, waiting for the manager, Walter Alston, to call him back to the dugout. Instead, Alston nodded for Maury to continue. Maury responded with another hit.

After eight and a half frustrating years, Maury finally found his "groove." The next day Maury got two hits, and four hits the day after that. His batting average soared.

In his first full season in the majors, Maury finally established himself as a major league shortstop and hitter, but he didn't stop there. He had yet to unleash his most natural talent—his God-given speed. Studying the motions of opposing pitchers, timing the throws of opposing catchers, practicing powerful takeoffs and deceptive slides, Maury started stealing bases like no one in the history of the game except for the great Hall of Famer Ty Cobb.

By his second season with the Dodgers, Maury led the league in base stealing. Base stealing had become Maury's own special weapon, distracting pitchers, causing wild throws by catchers, and drawing thousands of extra fans to the stadium to watch his magic. Most important, Maury was helping the Dodgers win games.

Even then, Maury wanted to accomplish more. He wouldn't be satisfied. He set his sights on Ty Cobb's record for stolen bases. In 1915, Cobb had stolen 96 bases in 156 games. Even though the regular baseball season in 1962 included 162 games, Maury's goal was to beat the record in 156 games, as Cobb had done. Maury began running like a man possessed. He slid into bases so many times he peeled the skin off his legs from hip to ankle. Bloody, bruised, bandaged, ignoring the pain, he never slowed down.

Game number 155 was in St. Louis against the Cardinals. Maury needed one steal to tie the record, two to break it. With every eye in the stadium on him, and the eyes of the nation watching on television, Maury got two hits and two steals. He broke a major league record that had stood for forty-seven years.

At the end of the season, Maury was named the Most Valuable Player in the National League, alongside Hall of Fame giants like Willie Mays, Don Drysdale, and Sandy Koufax.

The player who had once seemed stuck forever in the minor leagues, destined to end his career in mediocrity, had transformed himself into a bona fide star. All because, year after year, rejection after rejection, Maury Wills persisted, preparing himself. And when his moment came, when he had his chance to shine, he was ready.

■ **"Luck is opportunity meeting preparation."**

—Maury Wills

▪ Something to Think About ▪

During the 1984-85 season, the Los Angeles Lakers won the NBA championship over their great rivals, the Boston Celtics. But the next season, they suffered what Coach Pat Riley referred to as "the insidious disease of complacency," and they self-destructed in the Western Conference finals, losing to Houston. Coach Riley spent the summer with the coaching staff analyzing exactly what their team's weaknesses were and why they had lost, defining the areas where they needed to make improvement.

During the training camp for the new season, the coaches challenged each player to improve one percent above their career best in the five areas they identified most essential in playing the game of basketball. One percent may not sound like much, but if you take a dozen championship players and each one improves one percent in five key areas, the overall efficiency improvement adds up to 60%.

Because they focused on small, realistic goals, the players responded very positively. In fact, most players improved their games much more than one percent—some as much as 15, 20, even 50 percent. The Lakers won 67 games that season—including another NBA championship—and the next season became the first team in nineteen years to win back-to-back NBA titles.

·unstoppable·

"I hated every minute of the training, but I said, 'Don't quit. Suffer now and live the rest of your life as a champion.'"

—Muhammad Ali, Professional Boxer

■ UNSTOPPABLE ■

Being First Is Second Nature to This High Court Judge

Her Motto: Dogged Preparedness

Most future lawyers start thinking about law school as college undergraduates. A few of the more far-sighted start planning ahead in high school. But Leah Sears had her sights set on a law career at an age when most kids are thinking about a new bike or a pair of roller skates. When Leah was seven, she sent away for her first law school catalog.

Looking at the pictures in the catalogs, especially in those from Harvard and Yale, Leah noticed she didn't look like anyone there. Her skin was black, and almost every student she saw in the pictures was not only white, but male.

"I felt like I was a second-class citizen," she recalled. At that moment, a determination set in. "I knew I had to be somebody. And if that was to happen, I had to make things change." Not just for herself, but for others who had less than she had growing up in a middle-class military family. She wanted to make changes for people who needed more opportunities in life, who weren't part of the majority, who looked in the mirror and might see just a "nobody."

She knew if she was to succeed, she had to start now.

Supported and encouraged by her parents, Leah developed the confidence and drive to excel in school and participated fully in school activities. Her high school had never had an African-American cheerleader, but that didn't hold her back. She diligently rehearsed the routines and broke the school's color barrier when she was selected for the cheerleading team. Always, though, academics came first.

"Getting degrees from the best schools would be important to achieve my goal," she noted. "Because my parents couldn't afford to send me to those types of colleges, I was committed to getting an academic scholarship."

Her devotion paid off. She earned a full scholarship to Cornell University, graduated with honors in June of 1976, then completed her law studies at Emory University Law School in 1980. At twenty-five, she joined the prestigious Atlanta law firm of Alston and Bird, and although she found the experience rewarding, it involved "too much paperwork and not enough people work." The job was too far from her original goal. After two years, she left the firm to accept a much lower-paying position as a traffic judge in an Atlanta city court. The step felt right.

"I grew up at the intersection of the civil rights and women's rights movements and I saw the law making many changes for people like me," she commented. All her days of preparation had paid off. Now, with every step, she realized she would be breaking new ground. "There were very, very few black lawyers, and God knows no black female lawyers, so I had no mentor, no one to model myself after."

Because of her unique situation, she worked twice as hard at whatever she did. When she and her husband became parents in 1983 and again in 1986, she didn't let balancing her career and motherhood slow her down. When she campaigned for a superior court judgeship in 1988, her approach was simple: "I got three or four hours sleep a night from the time I announced I would run until the election." In a close three-way race, Leah became the youngest person and first African-American woman ever elected to the Georgia Superior Court.

Four years later, she took the biggest step of her life when Governor Zell Miller called personally to appoint her to the Georgia Supreme Court. Leah was thirty-six, the youngest person, the first woman, and the second African-American ever to sit on Georgia's highest court.

Yet with all her education, all her preparation, all her hard work, many dismissed her achievements as tokenism. "People didn't see me getting this job because I was a good judge; it was because I was a woman or because I was black," she said. She set out to prove them wrong but discovered yet another gap between her and the other justices: age. In one of her first days as a new justice, an older male judge made a comment about "the war." Leah remembered asking, "What war?" And he said, "World War II, the big one." In relating the incident, Leah said, "My war had been Vietnam, and it illustrated the type of a communication gap I faced. The judge leaned over to me and said bluntly, 'You're too damn young to be on a court like this!'"

"It was clear," Leah recollected. "I knew I had to work harder and be more prepared than any of the others to win the respect of my peers and the lawyers who practiced before me."

Leah made it a routine to arrive at her office every morning at 5:30, before anyone else, and carefully review her cases. She and her law clerks read every brief and met each morning to discuss them. Before the weekly meeting of the judges, she prepared everything she wanted to say in writing, never "winging it." After each meeting, she had her staff candidly review her performance. Before the next meeting, Leah focused on areas needing improvement.

"I was constantly talking to the other judges and asking them questions, eager to learn. I know I was a pain, but I never let up. Gradually, they started inviting me to lunch. One day, when I made a comment, they actually responded as if I was intelligent and had something to contribute. Then came the day when they actually listened to me."

Today, Justice Leah Sears is helping to make the changes she wanted to make as a child. She's changing the world, one case, one person at a time. "There's no doubt my success is the result of a lifetime of preparation and hard work. It's been a building process, and at any given point, I was prepared when the opportunity came."

■ **"There is no better way to dispel your critics than to be the most prepared and have your craft together. Know what you're talking about. Don't wing it. Excellence and thoroughness will always win people's respect."**

—Justice Leah Sears

▪ Something to Think About ▪

What do the following Hollywood superstars have in common?

Lucille Ball
Gary Cooper
Bill Cosby
Kevin Costner
Robert De Niro
Robert Duvall
Clark Gable
Teri Garr

Janet Gaynor
Whoopi Goldberg
Mark Harmon
Dustin Hoffman
Bob Hope
Casey Kasem
Michael Landon
Sophia Loren

Mary Tyler Moore
Ronald Reagan
Burt Reynolds
Tom Selleck
Suzanne Somers
Sylvester Stallone
Donald Sutherland
John Wayne
Marilyn Monroe

They all began their film careers at the bottom as extras.

(Source: People Entertainment Almanac)

UNSTOPPABLE

The Write Stuff

The Long Journey of a Short Story Writer

Rejection. It tumbles out of the mailbox, emerges oh-so-politely over the telephone receiver, and creeps out of the fax machine. Few writers escape rejection. Many have surrendered to it, but Noreen Ayres is not one of them. It took her thirty-five years, but in the end she proved that rejection is the rough draft of a success story.

Noreen had dreamed of being a writer since she was fourteen. An alert teacher had recognized her talent that year and suggested she plan to go to college. For Noreen, college was an astounding idea; no one in her family had ever graduated from high school, much less from college, and neither of her parents ever spoke of education.

The idea of a college education or a career would never have occurred to Noreen on her own. But the teacher lit a flame within her. She left home at seventeen, taking odd jobs to work her way through college.

At the university, her instructors saw something special in her writing, too. But before Noreen could develop her writing, she married and had a baby. Then began the countdown on her life: seven years as a full-time mother followed by eight years of taking college courses part time and earning a master's degree so she could teach. Working on and off at secretarial and teaching jobs, Noreen wrote poetry and short stories in her spare time. Years sped by, and she made only small inroads into the writing field. She found jobs as a proofreader and a technical writer. Six more years passed, but writing success eluded her. Her short stories won contests and drew encouraging letters from editors, but there was only one problem—no one published her stories.

Time was running out, and Noreen knew it. Long divorced from her first husband, she remarried at thirty-eight to Tom Glagola, another aspiring writer. They made two vows: their wedding vows and a vow to become published writers. Working full-time jobs, they wrote every spare moment they could. Yet after six years of effort, their work still remained unpublished. Feeling almost desperate, Noreen and her husband made a bold move and quit their jobs to pursue writing full time. To support themselves, they mortgaged their house. Even if they didn't succeed, they reasoned, they would have the satisfaction when they reached the age of sixty-five of knowing they had given writing their best shot.

Noreen wrote story after story and submitted them everywhere she could. The clock ticked on. A year and a half passed without a single piece being published. Discouragement set in. She wondered if she didn't have what it took after all. She was at a pivotal moment—the moment when a person either gives up the dream or decides to fight for it with every ounce of will and spirit. Noreen Ayres decided to fight.

She joined a writers' group. Fueled by the encouragement and feedback of the group's members, Noreen turned to writing mystery novels. Her first "whodunit" went out to thirty-three agents, and thirty-three rejection letters came back. She sent the manuscript to three publishers, and three rejections followed. She heard praise for her style but not for her storytelling skills. Turning rejections into a learning opportunity, Noreen enrolled in courses on criminal investigation and forensic science, collected crime articles from periodicals, and interviewed professionals in the field. One day she learned of a case that tugged at her heart. It was the story of a hard-working convenience store clerk who had been brutally murdered in a robbery. Moved and intrigued, Noreen sat down to write.

Noreen took the first hundred pages to a writers' conference that literary agents would also be attending. Before the conference, Noreen prepared carefully, researching each agent's background and level of success. At the conference, she showed her manuscript to her first choice, a representative from the prestigious William Morris Agency.

This time there was no rejection. The agent asked just one simple question: "How much do you want for an advance?" The customary advance for an unpublished writer is usually $5,000 to $7,000. Noreen didn't know that, so she blurted out an amount that would allow her to write full time for two years: "$150,000." The agent said he'd get back to her. A few days later he called to say that the publisher hadn't met her demand. Instead, they offered $120,000 and a contract for two books, a deal almost unheard of for a new writer.

Noreen was fifty-two when she finally became a published writer. Her first book, *A World the Color of Salt*, published in 1992, received rave reviews and gathered a dedicated following. *Carcass Trade*, her second book, was published in 1994, and she recently completed her third, *The Juan Doe Murders*.

Although Noreen wrote for more than three decades before her work was published, she ultimately achieved her goal. No one can predict what Noreen will write in the future, but it will not be about regrets.

■ **"A writer cannot choose when or if success will come. You can only do your best and be prepared for your moment of opportunity by writing, writing, writing—and then writing some more."**

—Noreen Ayres

UNSTOPPABLE

"This is just a prelude to going back for my doctorate."

.unstoppable.

"There is no substitute for hard work.
There will be disappointments,
but 'the harder you work,
the luckier you will get.'
Never be satisfied with less
than your very best effort.
If you strive for the top and miss,
you'll still 'beat the pack.'"

—Gerald R. Ford, Thirty-eighth President

▪ In Their Own Words ▪

***"My mother was a young girl** of 19 when I was born so I was raised by my grandparents in a farming town in North Carolina. I was a fat child, pigeon-toed, and as a result fell down all of the time. I also had a speech impediment. When I spoke it sounded like I had rocks in my mouth and everybody laughed because they couldn't understand what I said. I spent most of my childhood hiding behind my grandmother's apron.*

"At school, it only got worse. I realized I didn't talk like other kids and they teased me until I didn't want to speak a word. Fortunately, I had two teachers who found me, and then helped me find my voice.

"The first was Miss Phar. She was just out of college and a very creative young woman, although I didn't see her that way at first. She asked us to write a story and then read it in front of the class. I felt like that assignment was a slap in the face. I had been laughed at and picked at constantly, and I didn't think I could take any more embarrassment, especially the children mocking me as I read my story in front of the entire class. After hearing my pleas, she said that if I wrote a great story—with all the i's dotted and all t's crossed—she would read the story for me. So I did.

"It worked so well, I started writing lots of stories and poems. I figured if I could impress the teachers by being creative and do a little extra, they wouldn't notice my speech impediment. Soon my fellow students started coming to me to ask what they could write about. That lifted my self-esteem because they stopped laughing when they had to ask me a question.

"But my life really changed when I was 14. My baby brother handed me a glass bottle one day and accidentally smacked me in the

face. My mouth swelled up and my teeth got loose in the gums. Three or four weeks later, they turned black and my mom took me to the dentist. He examined my mouth and discovered something was not right—I had two sets of impacted teeth in my mouth. He told me that's why I had trouble talking. He also told me it could be fixed.

"He pulled all the teeth from my upper jaw and fitted me for false teeth, but the roof of my mouth was disfigured and scarred and I still had trouble speaking when I started high school that fall. In my English class, the teacher called on me to read and when she heard me struggling, she asked if I would come to see her after school. Her name was Abna Aggrey Lancaster. I told her about my false teeth and that I didn't want anyone else to find out. She suggested I come to her class every afternoon to do a little work.

"It turned out to be a lot of work—every afternoon for four years. She made me memorize and recite poems and Shakespeare soliloquies. She made me work on every word. I learned not only how to speak, but how to stand, how to breathe and how to speak from the diaphragm. Every day I walked to her classroom I'd secretly hope she wouldn't be there. She always was.

"My senior year, I stood on a stage and recited a monologue called 'A Mother's Love' for an oratorical contest. When I finished, the entire high school stood up and applauded. It made me grin inside because here I was winning first prize for the same thing people had been laughing at for most of my life.

"Ironically, it was my most serious impediment—the inability to speak—that helped me develop my greatest gift. But I will never forget how much work was involved to reach this point, and how long it took.

"I believe that all of us have the potential to rise above our weaknesses, and even to use those weaknesses as foundations for our

success. If we are willing to diligently practice and develop the skills, we can be successful in whatever field we choose."

Jackie Torrence

Jackie Torrence is a professional story teller who travels throughout the world to share her stories with enthusiastic listeners in storytelling festivals, colleges and universities, radio and television.

Your Personal Action Plan

Preparing for Your Future

The will to win is important; the will to plan is vital. That's what a college football coach once said, and his team's victories on the field proved him right.

Most people want to win. They want the rewards, glory, and satisfaction of achievement. Yet, tragically, few people take it to the next level and actually plan for that success. Planning doesn't have the glamour of winning. Planning is hard work with no immediate payoff. But without a plan you leave your future to the whimsy of fate—a victim of circumstance. With a plan, you are the captain of your life: you determine the direction of your future.

Most people have no plan for their lives. Many have an idea that they'll work a certain number of years, then retire. Some may have fantasies and hopes, but they do not have plans. Instead, they respond to what life brings according to the needs of the day. People may have innovative ideas but then might scrutinize them over and over until they find all the reasons why their ideas will not work. Others forge ahead before they are ready. Such people might start a business before they identify their target markets, determine the best location, or calculate the financial resources required to keep their businesses afloat until they become established.

You may know people who have changed their jobs or even their careers—usually for financial benefits—without first considering whether or not they will enjoy the new work or even determining that the field is one that they want to pursue. This sort of movement can waste enormous amounts of time, energy, and money. As I mentioned in chapter one, I found myself in this position, spending lots of time and money pursuing things that ultimately weren't in line with my purpose or passion. Fortunately, I shifted my efforts toward determining what mattered most to me and then pursued only those opportunities.

The following steps will help you prepare your personal plan of action.

Step 1: Identify the Desired Result

The first step in designing a plan is to look ahead at the end result you envision. By developing a clear vision of what you ultimately want to achieve, it will be easier to identify the steps to get there.

> **Action:** Write a clear and concise statement of specifically what you want to accomplish and by what date. Make sure the statement is consistent with your purpose and passion.

Step 2: Determine the Skills You'll Need

Unstoppable people are willing to become students. They exert the energy and make the sacrifices necessary to educate themselves and to acquire the knowledge and skills necessary to fulfill their dreams. This education may involve returning to school or taking classes at night. You may also have to invest months—even years—in research. Many people take training or pursue new jobs that broaden their experience and knowledge. Without exception, you must have an unwavering commitment to do *whatever is necessary* to become fully prepared for the tasks ahead.

From the greatest achievements to the most personal accomplishments, preparation is essential to success. To become a physician, one must first take pre-med courses, attend medical school, and complete a residency before starting to practice medicine. Musicians develop their talents by practicing daily for hours, year after year. People in business spend years acquiring skills that may involve taking evening classes, attending seminars and conferences, or earning undergraduate or graduate degrees.

Tip: If you're currently working for a large company, take advantage of the wealth of opportunities available for learning. The educational resources offered by companies are substantial. Many companies offer training and will pay at least a portion, if not all of the costs for continuing education, undergraduate, and graduate courses.

During the ten years I worked for Sprint, I completed my bachelor of science degree in business administration and took courses toward a master's degree in business administration. Additionally, I attended hundreds of hours of seminars and in-house training, including courses in selling, negotiation, problem solving, presentation skills, project management, and management skills. By investing my time, I improved my skills and knowledge as a Sprint employee, thereby benefiting the company. I was also growing as an individual, and each step further prepared me for the endeavors I am now pursuing.

Action: Research and identify the skills, education, and experience required to achieve your goal. One way to help you learn about those requirements is to talk to people who are doing what you want to do.

STEP 3: CREATE A PLAN OF ACTION

By their very nature, dreams have a tendency to be broad and vague. To be unstoppable, you must convert your dream into reality. You can do so easily by taking your goal and breaking it into smaller steps. Then arrange the steps in priority order and write dates next to each step indicating when it must be accomplished to meet your ultimate objective. A clear, methodical approach will help you move steadily forward, without danger of being overwhelmed by the ultimate goal.

Using my goal as an example, I have included a few excerpts from my action plan to demonstrate the three steps.

- **Identify the desired result:**
  To write the first in a series of best-selling books. The book's goal is to inspire and instruct people on how to become aware of the greater possibilities for their own lives and how to take action to achieve them. *Unstoppable*, the first title, will be published in spring 1998.

- **Determine the skills needed:**
  1. Researching
  2. Interviewing
  3. Writing/editing skills

- **Create a plan of action:**
  Researching
  1. Hire an individual who has research skills to assist in locating the unstoppable people for my book. (January 1996)

2. Select unstoppable individuals to include (March 1996)
3. Interview participants. (March through June 1996)

Interviewing

1. Identify and read books on interviewing.
2. Speak to other writers and get their feedback on how to best schedule and conduct interviews.
3. Hire individual to type transcripts of interviews.

Writing/editing

1. Hire an individual with experience in developing and editing books. (January 1996)
2. Write the book. (June through December 1996)
3. Edit the book. (January and February 1997)

Along the way, I modified many of these tasks and schedules. However, the action plan was an invaluable tool in helping me achieve my goals. The completion of this book is one step forward in my ultimate journey and proof that writing a plan and following it works.

Action: Now it's time for you to create your unstoppable plan of action.

1. Write a clear and concise statement of specifically what you want to accomplish and by what date.
2. Break your goal down into single steps and activities.
3. Prioritize the steps and write dates next to each indicating when each step must be accomplished to meet your ultimate objective.
4. Review your action plan daily.
5. Do at least one thing every day to move yourself closer to your goal.

Many of you have written plans and are well on your way to accomplishing your goals. Some of you are just realizing what what it is you really want. Regardless of what you want to accomplish, it begins with a dream. But without a plan, your dream may remain just a dream.

Start now! Put together your action plan. Then, remember the action part.

■ **"The heights by great men reached and kept**
Were not attained by sudden flight,
But they, while their companions slept,
Were toiling upward in the night."

—Henry Wadsworth Longfellow

Characteristic Five

TEAMS
Strengthen the Cause

Although pursuing your dreams may feel lonely at times, it doesn't have to. The unstoppable people you will encounter next built a support team of friends, family, colleagues, advisors, and mentors who were with them all the way. If they didn't have supporters when they started, these people went out and found them. They assembled their team, sometimes small, sometimes large, but always strong enough to support them emotionally and knowledgeable enough to guide them toward success.

You don't have to do it alone and you shouldn't. The stronger your team, the more unstoppable you become.

"Your Personal Action Plan" will reveal the best places for you to find inspirational role models and mentors and how to easily develop your own personal "dream team."

■ **"You can make it, but it's easier if you don't have to do it alone."**

—Betty Ford

■ UNSTOPPABLE ■

Words Failed Him

Until He Learned to Ask for Help

The judging committee gave Tom Harken one of the most prestigious awards in America, without even realizing the reason he most deserved it. It was the Horatio Alger Award—given each year to individuals who have overcome tremendous adversity to achieve greatness in their fields. But not until Tom's brave and startling acceptance speech did the audience or the judging committee realize how great that adversity had been. That night, Tom Harken confessed a secret he'd been hiding for almost fifty years.

Tom Harken, entrepreneur, self-made millionaire, and owner and franchisee of Casa Olé restaurants, confessed publicly that he had been illiterate nearly all his life. While most children were learning to decipher "See Spot Run," Tom was in the hospital. He had polio and was confined to an iron lung for a year. Then, after returning home from the hospital, he contracted tuberculosis and was quarantined in his room for eight months. Years passed, and Tom fell further and further behind in his school work.

Upon his eventual return to school, an insensitive teacher mocked Tom when he couldn't recognize the simple word "cat." That teacher shattered his confidence. Tom dropped out of school and relied instead on what his father called "an ability to talk good and work hard."

In later years, he was able to rely on something else too: the support of Melba, his bright, encouraging wife. Miss Melba, as he likes to call her, knew before they married that her husband was illiterate. She found out when he told her she'd have to fill out the application for a marriage license.

Tom started working as a door-to-door vacuum cleaner salesman in Oklahoma. When he made a sale, he memorized the client's name and address, employer, and credit information. When he arrived home, many times late at night after the children had been put to bed, he called on his highly developed memory and repeated the detailed information to Melba, who completed the necessary forms.

Tireless and determined, he sometimes knocked on a hundred doors a day before selling one vacuum cleaner. He worked so hard he was named to the Kirby Vacuum Cleaner Company's Hall of Fame. But he still couldn't read.

After several years, always with Melba's support and encouragement, Tom purchased a recreational vehicle dealership. He became the top selling independent broker in the business. He still couldn't write. His next venture was to open the first of what eventually would become a chain of twelve restaurants. Yet he couldn't even read his own menu.

When he ate out, he always ordered a cheeseburger, assuming it was something every restaurant offered. It worked for years until one day a waitress snapped, "What's the matter, can't you read? We don't serve cheeseburgers." It was one of the countless humiliations Tom experienced almost every day of his life.

Yet the greatest sadness Tom experienced was not in restaurants but at home in his easy chair, when his two sons climbed on his lap and asked him to read the comics to them. Quickly, Melba would intercede, telling the boys their father was too busy, and she would read to them instead. His sons grew to adulthood, became businessmen themselves, and never knew their father was illiterate.

Tom couldn't read the signs on freeways, but he sure could read the signs of his life. He knew that until he learned to read, he would never be completely free or happy. He set off then on the hardest venture of his life, his journey toward literacy. The first, most painful step was to ask for help. "Nothing is impossible," he said, "if you're humble enough and desperate enough to get the right people to help you." The right person, the logical one to ask, was the one who had always believed in him, his wife. Melba taught him to read, word by word, night after night. It took years, and Tom was not an easy student; he became frustrated and sometimes angry. But he persevered, and continually improved, first reading simple sentences and then long passages from the Bible.

When he was told he would receive the Horatio Alger Award, Tom Harken was thrilled. After much thought, he resolved to go public about the secret he and Melba had kept for so long. He hoped it might encourage other illiterate Americans to learn to read and lift the burden of shame from his own shoulders.

First, though, he told his two sons. They were stunned. But their reaction was nothing compared to that of the audience at the Horatio Alger Awards ceremony. Hundreds of men and women, the top achievers in every field, listened in silence as Tom confessed his complete illiteracy, which had ended only recently.

At the close of his speech, the audience rose to their feet in applause, then crowded forward to shake the hand of the man who had moved so many of them to tears.

Tom Harken, like most achievers, does not regret the hardships of his past. It was those hardships, he said, that revealed his strength. Now he shares that strength with others. He's given more than 500 speeches about the importance of literacy to both children and adults, encouraging them to begin the same journey he did. He tells them they may get lost sometimes along the way they may become confused and angry, but there will always be someone willing to guide them from word to word, from shame to pride.

■ **"Will you help me? Those are the only words you need to say, and someone will help you."**

—Tom Harken

·unstoppable·

"You can't do it all yourself.
Don't be afraid to rely on others
to help you accomplish your goals."

—Oprah Winfrey

▪ UNSTOPPABLE ▪

He Achieved the Impossible

With a Little Help from His Friends

Iqbal Masih spent his childhood shackled to a loom in a dingy carpet factory in Pakistan. At the age of four, when his parents hired him out to repay a $16 loan, he worked twelve- to sixteen-hour days, seven days a week, for less than a dollar a month. He never learned to read or write and was thin and undernourished.

Craig Kielburger spent his childhood in the comfortable suburbs of Toronto raised by two loving parents who were both teachers. During the day he attended school. In his free time, he spent his boundless energy in-line skating, swimming, and skiing.

Two boys from two entirely different worlds—until the year they both turned twelve. The impoverished child of the East and the privileged child of the West were symbolically united in a universal effort to liberate enslaved children.

Iqbal was rescued from his factory prison when he was ten. For the next two years, he was treated as an international hero, a living symbol in a brave crusade against bonded servitude in

Pakistan's carpet industry. Then, at the age of twelve, Iqbal was murdered, his voice forever silenced.

Halfway across the world, Craig Kielburger read the story about Iqbal's life and death in his local newspaper. At that moment, Craig's carefree days of childhood ended. Fueled by compassion and a sense of justice, Craig vowed to do everything he could to help end the exploitation of child workers. He had the intelligence and foresight to know he couldn't do it alone, that he would have to rally others to his cause. People told him he was too young. They said no one would listen to him. But Craig Kielburger, at the age of twelve, was an effective activist. He knew how to unite others to work toward the same goal.

He read everything he could find about the 200 million children in the world who work in conditions of slavery. But reading wasn't enough. Craig wanted to see for himself the children and the conditions they worked in. At first, his parents refused. After all, Craig wasn't even old enough to take the subway downtown alone. But Craig was determined. He sold some of his toys to raise money for the trip. His parents were so moved by Craig's determination that they granted their permission for his seven-week trip to Asia and, with help from other relatives, matched the money he raised.

Armed with a video camera and chaperoned at each stop by local human-rights activists, Craig traveled from Bangladesh to Thailand and on to India, Nepal, and Pakistan. He made his way from windowless sweatshops to airless factories. He met a little girl bagging candy eleven hours a day in a stuffy, overheated room and a little barefoot boy stitching soccer balls. He talked to each one, child to child, and the children opened up like they never had before. At the end of his journey, Craig made a pilgrimage to the place where Iqbal's own journey had ended, an unmarked grave in a small cemetery.

While Craig was touring Asia, the prime minister of Canada was also there. Craig requested a meeting with the prime minister, but he refused. After all, Craig was just a child, too young to vote. The media however, was very interested in hearing Craig and two former child laborers tell their stories. The subsequent coverage outraged the public; overnight, the issue of child labor received national attention in Canada. Suddenly, the prime minister wanted to see Craig too.

Craig knew now what he had to do, but he could not accomplish his goal alone. He needed a team. What better partners, he thought, than his classmates who, like himself, were "too young to know any better." Back home, Craig took his shocking photos and horrifying stories into classrooms. Craig said, "Here's the problem. Do you want to help?" His fellow students were more than eager to help. Together they established a group called Free the Children, which met weekly to share information and discuss strategies. Craig then contacted other organizations for further information, support, and contacts. His team was growing.

After hearing Craig speak at the Ontario Federation of Labor's annual convention, 2,000 union leaders joined the effort, donating $150,000 to Free the Children. The mayor of Toronto banned fireworks made in child-labor shops. The minister of foreign affairs offered Craig an advisory position in the Canadian government, and the United States Congress invited him to speak. The Canadian government has now become one of the leading nations working toward the elimination of intolerable forms of child labor and the exploitation of children.

"Children have one special quality that gives them a far greater power than adults," Craig said. "They have imagination. They still think they can fly. They even think they can talk to prime ministers as equals."

In two short years, Free the Children became a team of thousands, expanding into an international movement with chapters across Europe and Asia. Free the Children has changed minds. It has changed laws, and it has begun to change the lives of 200 million children.

Kid stuff? You decide.

■ **"It's easier to be ignorant and say I don't know about the problem. But once you know, once you've seen it in their eyes, then you have a responsibility to do something. There is strength in numbers, and if we all work together as a team, we can be unstoppable."**

—Craig Kielburger

UNSTOPPABLE
GEORGE CRENSHAW

·unstoppable·

"The young do not know enough to be prudent, and therefore they attempt the impossible—and achieve it, generation after generation."

—Pearl S. Buck

UNSTOPPABLE

Mother Knows Best

How a Matriarch Built a Business Family and Saved the Family Business

Gertrude Boyle is the seventy-year-old chairwoman of the board and the guiding spirit behind Columbia Sportswear, the world's largest manufacturer of outdoor apparel. But Gert didn't rise to the top of the business world like most executives. Tragedy forced her into the corporate arena, and the team-building instincts she had developed as a mother helped her to survive and even to succeed.

She learned survival skills early, when her Jewish family fled Germany during Adolf Hitler's ominous rise to power. In the United States, her father founded the Columbia Hat Company in Portland, Oregon, which he passed on to Gert's husband, Neal, in the mid-1960s. Neal built the company into a small outlet for hunting and fishing clothes while Gert occupied herself with raising their three children. Then Neal suffered a fatal heart attack only three months after he'd taken out a $150,000 Small Business Administration (SBA) loan. For collateral, he'd put up their home, their beach house, Gert's mother's home, and his life insurance policy.

At forty-seven, Gert faced major problems. When Neal died, she knew almost nothing about the business. Yet the day after his funeral, Gert called a meeting at the plant, asking Columbia's forty employees to help her keep the business going. Filling her husband's shoes as the company's president proved a formidable challenge. Over the next few months, she frequently heard comments like, "Your husband wouldn't have done it that way!" The company's long-time lawyer and accountant both encouraged her to give up the business. "Come on, Gert, you're a woman. You don't know how to run this thing." But to quit would mean giving up everything her husband had built, along with her family's financial stability.

So Gert dug in. She fired the attorney and accountant and every other naysayer within the company. She asked her son Tim to come home from the University of Oregon on weekends and help out. The challenge was more than either had anticipated. "Together, we nearly ran Columbia into the ground. We made every mistake in the book and fired everyone who knew anything about our business," she admitted. And the books showed it. Sales dropped $200,000 the first year.

Weary and defeated, with her banker ready to call in the SBA loan, Gert considered selling the company. But the prospective buyer was willing to pay her only $1,400 and planned to break up the company. Gert was appalled: $1,400 for the family's labor of thirty years! "What the heck," she told him. "For $1,400, I'll drive it into the ground myself!"

Gert made a new commitment to save Columbia and mustered all the grit she had into rebuilding the business. But to save the company she knew she would need a team to support her. Gert first appealed to her employees, encouraging their input, and implemented an employee incentive plan based on the company's success. She then put up the company's building as collateral on the loan; and the bank not only backed off on its threats but became a much-needed ally. Her banker recommended that she speak with another of the bank's clients, Ron Nelson, who worked for Nike, a nearby up-and-coming shoe company. Impressed with Gert's dedication, Ron joined Columbia's board of directors, donating his time. Ron joining the board was a turning point for Columbia because every problem Columbia faced was one that Ron and Nike had already experienced. With Ron's insight, and Columbia's fully supportive, hard-working group of employees, Gert kept Columbia afloat through its most difficult years.

She took another risk when she put her son Tim—despite his lack of experience—in charge of selling to national retailers. Tim discovered Columbia was losing money by distributing products manufactured by other companies and suggested the company identify a niche market that would allow Columbia to shift its focus to its own line, which emphasized high quality outdoor gear at affordable prices.

That new focus led Columbia to become the first company to use the breathable, water-repellent Gore-tex fabric that revolutionized sportswear. Columbia also introduced the now famous Bugaboo parka with a removable fleece lining. The parka was half the price of similar jackets and quickly outsold the competition. Gert then expanded the sportswear line to include everything from snow pants to shoes.

Through all this, Gert was still battling the old-boy's club mentality that dominates so much of the business world. Because she was a woman, one caller refused to believe she was the company's president and kept demanding to speak to someone higher up. Finally, Gert informed the stubborn man, "Sorry, God is busy."

In the end, Gert found a unique way to capitalize on her womanhood. She approved an ad campaign designed to exploit the image of "a little old lady running the company." The commercials featured her as Mother Gert, an overbearing nag who pushed son Tim to absurd lengths to test the ruggedness of their products. In one ad she forced him to walk through a carwash to show their jackets are waterproof. Another showed Tim "accidentally" pushing his scowling mother off a cliff, then rescuing her by knotting together the shell and liner of his parka and pulling her to safety.

"Experts" warned that macho men would not accept the image of a nagging mother telling them what to wear. Gert went ahead with the self-deprecating campaign anyway, and consumers fell off their sofas laughing. The ad campaign was a huge success, and sales climbed from $10 million in 1982 to over $360 million in 1995.

Although Tim Boyle took over as CEO in 1989, his visionary mother remains actively involved in all important company decisions and much of its promotion. Today, Columbia Sportswear owns approximately 30 percent of the outdoor apparel market and growth has averaged 40 percent annually. *BusinessWeek* has praised Gertrude as one of the nation's best managers and *Working Woman* named her as one of America's top women business owners.

Most importantly, behind all the accolades is a woman who saved her family's business by building a business family.

■ **"If you don't know something, don't be afraid to ask for help."**

—Gertrude Boyle

.unstoppable.

"I have developed over the years a whole group of important people, people important to me that I consider mentors. Now, they may be the gardener in the estate down the road. They may be a farmer who milks his cows.
They may be a very special professor. It may be someone I've never met, but only read about...like [author Gabriel] Garcia Marquez. One of my dreams is to meet him. But those are my mentors. George Eliot, the great novelist. Jane Austen is a mentor of mine, in terms of language. So, I've informally constructed this structure in my life of mentors."

—*Martha Stewart*

■ UNSTOPPABLE ■

He Failed to Make the Grade in School

But His Team Concept Helped Him Build a Business Empire

Readin', writin', and 'rithmetic. The three Rs are the foundation of all education. The essentials for success in life. At least that's what we've always been told. Paul Orfalea made his way through school proficient in only one out of the three—but that didn't stop him from becoming one of the most remarkable business success stories of the latter twentieth century.

For Paul, the printed page has always been his greatest obstacle. He flunked second grade because he didn't know his ABCs. His reading and spelling were so poor he was pulled out of public school in the third grade and placed in a special class with slow learners. Six weeks later, his mother had him tested and learned that her son wasn't mentally deficient after all. In fact, he had an IQ of 128. She immediately took him out of that class, but her only option was to put him back into the public school system. Endless visits to eye doctors and reading specialists didn't offer any answers. Unfortunately, the world still had a lot to learn about dyslexia.

Fortunately, Paul had strong support from his parents. "While everyone else around me made me feel stupid, my parents were always on my side. They joked that they had to spend $50 on tutors and special classes for every word I learned to read, but they never blamed me. They only offered encouragement."

Despite his limited success in school, Paul said he still felt good about himself because he could play chess and other games really well. At an early age, Paul showed a fascination with the stock market. His father, who was in the clothing business, had taught Paul the importance of saving and investing money. When Paul was eight, his father helped him buy his first stock. Throughout his school years, Paul continued investing his allowance.

When Paul finally graduated from high school, he ranked near the bottom of his class. He'd been fired from his job as a fountain boy for misreading orders. He'd lasted only one day pumping gas because his boss couldn't read his handwriting on the charge slips.

"I was convinced that I was unemployable," Paul said. "I also realized that if I wanted to do anything significant with my life, I'd need the help of others."

As a teenager, that help came from two of Paul's cousins. The cousins had decided to earn money by painting address numbers on the curbs in front of homes, and while Paul couldn't be in charge of painting the numbers in the right order, he could certainly sell the service door-to-door. The business folded abruptly when the three found out they hadn't used quick-dry paint, and their numbers were running into the gutter.

The three then tried their hands at running a roadside vegetable stand—with more success. That summer, Paul learned something that would set the course for his future business. "My father made women's clothes and I sold vegetables. Over time, the vegetables would rot and the clothes would go out of style," Paul recollected. "I realized that I didn't want to run any business that had inventory."

While keeping his eye out for the right business opportunity, graduating from college became an important goal for Paul. He didn't want to feel inferior to anyone. In order to get accepted at the University of Southern California (USC), he'd have to earn a B average in community college. This goal was formidable since Paul had barely graduated from high school. But he enrolled in his local community college and earned that B average with the support of friends, tutors, and a little ingenuity. He took courses that focused on his strengths—algebra, geometry, and finance—and used creativity to get through the others. He took a class in "Great Plays" instead of a traditional literature course that required reading seventeen books—a lifetime of reading for someone with dyslexia. And he postponed freshman English until his last course at USC where he barely earned a D.

Paul entered the University of Southern California where he majored in finance and graduated with a C average. While he was at the university, Paul discovered the business he had been looking for.

"I was assigned to a study group to work on a class project, but because of my dyslexia, I couldn't read or help with the paper," he recalled. "I made a deal with the other students that if they would write the paper, I would be the group's 'gofer.'" Paul spent hours at the campus library making copies for his group and became intrigued by the copy machine. Copy machines were a fairly new development in the early 1970s, and as Paul observed, "The machine operated so simply. All you had to do was plug it in."

Just as importantly, as a business, photocopying required no inventory.

Paul had studied product life cycles in a marketing class and felt certain that photocopying was going to revolutionize document reproduction in the decades ahead. In his fifth year in college, he borrowed $5,000 from a bank, rented a former hamburger stand near the university, and set up a small photocopy shop for students.

Again, Paul quickly realized that he needed the help of others to make the business a reality. Operating and maintaining machines were not exactly his forte. Paul quickly found a local student who was blessed with the mechanical skills that he lacked and took the student on as a partner.

They charged 4¢ a page—well below the dime-a-page charge in the campus library—and the little business boomed. "I knew I had a concept that would work on any campus," Paul said. "To help me open and finance new locations, I took in partners who put up cash and gave me a controlling interest in each store. This allowed me to expand rapidly without the need for outside capital." Building partnerships became a key factor in the growth of Paul's business.

In the beginning, Paul found fellow students who wanted to become a part of his team. He required a minimal initial investment and encouraged them to drive up and down the West Coast and open new locations near colleges with enrollments of 20,000 students or more.

In addition to finding partners to share in the risk and success of his business, Paul established a company culture that fostered self-respect and motivation. Paul never liked the term "employee" or "subordinate" or the idea of working for someone. Because of his philosophy, all employees were referred to as co-workers—everyone from the front-line person running the cash register to the co-owner/partner. And everyone shared in the profits. Paul's goal was to make the co-workers feel like valued members of the team and have, what he called, "happy fingers"—the knowledge that as co-workers rang up sales, they were benefiting personally.

But the team concept didn't stop there. Paul developed strategic alliances with premiere vendors such as Xerox, Kodak, and Sprint. By working together, Paul could supply his stores with upgradable, state-of-the-art equipment that was leased rather than purchased. This arrangement minimized the need for capital and ultimately allowed Paul's business to stay ahead of the competition.

By 1990, there were 480 Kinko's stores making copies across the United States. In just seven short years, that number has grown to 850 locations worldwide, with 23,000 co-workers and 200,000 business customers every day. Amazingly, until January 1997, Paul and his partners had no outside investors, and the company remained privately held. Kinko's brought in an outside investor to help finance an aggressive expansion plan. The investment firm holds approximately 30 percent of the company's equity. Paul and his partners have most of the remaining 70 percent.

"It's never been easy. In the twenty-seven years Kinko's has been in business, we've had competitors beating down our doors and we never had enough cash to implement the hundreds of ideas we'd like to. It's a miracle we were able to keep the company private for twenty-seven years," Paul pointed out. "I didn't achieve that alone. I recognized the need early in life to have capable, motivated people around me and to create a team environment so that everyone could share in its success."

Paul Orfalea may not have mastered his readin' and writin'. He may not have been blessed with mechanical skills. But he understood the value of bringing the right people together to make things happen and the value of a partnership and a team. In doing so, he created the largest retail provider of document management and business services in the world.

■ "My motto has always been that anybody can do it better than me. By enlisting the support of others and giving them equity in the business, I was able to focus on my strengths and develop a business that benefited everyone."

—Paul Orfalea

I know my grades are lousy but you always said, "It's not what you know, it's who you know."

UNSTOPPABLE

Going for the Gold

Friendship Takes a City to Olympian Heights

He was a real estate lawyer with no experience in professional management. He had never traveled abroad on business. His only experience with sports was playing college football twenty years ago. And the city where he lived wasn't exactly an international hub or hot spot.

So what made Billy Payne think he could possibly bring the 1996 Summer Olympics—the largest international sporting event in history—to the little-known city of Atlanta?

"Friends," he said. "Friendship will sustain an effort and an idea long before rationality will support it."

In fact, even some of Billy's friends wondered if he was rational when he came up with the crazy idea on February 8, 1987. Billy was in church that day, dedicating a new sanctuary for which he had helped raise funds. The people around him had worked and sacrificed, believing they could raise $2 million for the project. When the costs exceeded the estimates, they had reached even deeper, financially and spiritually. Billy saw people who had been honored and delighted to continue giving money to build a dream.

And here they were today, sharing joy and a sense of success.

He turned to his wife, Martha, and said, "Wouldn't it be great if the entire city could experience what we've experienced here in our church today? Let's think of a way to do that."

His first ideas—a Super Bowl and a Democratic convention—were already on the city's agenda. Billy Payne decided he had to think bigger. *The friendliness of the people in the South combined with the Olympic Games, what could be better?*

The next available Olympics was 1996, but that would be the 100th anniversary of the games, and everyone expected them to be held in Athens, Greece, the site of the original Olympics 2,500 years ago. Second on the list of likely choices was Toronto, which offered tremendous resources. If Atlanta bid for the Olympics, it would be the city's first bid. Since the games had resumed after World War II, the International Olympic Committee (IOC) had never chosen a city applying for the first time.

Atlanta didn't seem to have a chance. But it did have Billy Payne. He had drive and intensity and loved competition, but not in the same way he had expressed these characteristics for most of his life.

"I was so competitive as an adolescent and young adult that I took competitiveness to a fault. As a consequence, I woke up one day when I was around thirty and realized I didn't have many friends," Billy remembered. After discussing this insight with his wife, he made a list of things he wanted to be competitive about and the areas of his life where friendship and relationships meant more than winning. "Almost overnight I started having more friends. And I also noticed that as a consequence of having more friends, the opportunities in my professional life—what I sought to do and was asked to do civically—increased rather dramatically. At the end of the day, people want to associate with their friends."

But it took a heart attack in 1982 for Billy to make the biggest change in his life. Faced with his own mortality, he decided to spend his time in a conscious effort to do something that would potentially contribute to the greatest good.

"The most important thing about establishing goals is to make sure they are important to other people in addition to you," Billy said. "In other words, there's a great tendency to be self-serving—'I want to have the biggest house,' 'I want to be head of the company,' 'I want to make the most money.' What in fact brings joy in life is a goal that while it benefits and motivates you it also benefits others."

Bringing the Olympics to Atlanta certainly fit those criteria. Now he would need to get his friends to share his vision. The first night, his wife encouraged him to call his friend Peter Candler, believing he might talk Billy out of his Olympic idea. Surprising them both, Peter not only supported the idea, he also suggested Billy contact several key businesswomen in Atlanta who could help broaden the appeal of his effort and reach different constituencies in the community.

By March, Billy's Olympic team had grown to four. In an act of commitment, Billy left his law partnership to devote himself full time to his crusade. He supported his family by taking out a loan against income property he owned. Billy knew his next step was to get people with political power enrolled in his effort. Peter suggested contacting an old friend, Horace Sibley, who, in turn, might connect him with Mayor Andrew Young. But Horace's associates and assistants had heard about Billy's crazy idea and tried to protect Horace from it. Billy finally got his foot in the door, first with Horace, then with Young, but he could tell that both men thought his idea was outrageous.

"I could tell the mayor wasn't buying it, so I shifted gears in the middle of our first conversation," Billy said. He knew Young had been a former ambassador to the United Nations, as well as a famed civil rights leader. Billy's Olympic idea would also have to have civic appeal. "I started talking about the legacy that would come from the attempt whether or not we were successful—how I thought it could inspire a youth sports movement in our own community, how it could do some good."

Young remembered being impressed with Billy's single-minded dedication. The mayor saw a man who had quit his job, mortgaged his property, and started living on his savings to achieve a goal that seemed impossible or, at best, highly improbable. Billy talked about fund-raising and how the city wouldn't need new taxes because he believed corporations would be happy to give once they, too, shared the dream.

"By the time I said, 'Don't worry, it's not going to cost the city any money,' the mayor was hooked."

By June, with Young on board, Billy's dream team was now known as the "Atlanta Nine." The "Nine" went to every corner of the city looking for support: The *Atlanta Journal-Constitution* called it a "nutty dream" and labeled the effort a long-shot; sports marketing companies thought the group had absolutely lost their minds; and even the Chamber of Commerce said it was a wonderful idea but that there was no way the Chamber would put the hard-earned money of corporate Atlanta behind an idea with "zero possibility."

"The skepticism and criticism were directed more at the magnitude of the idea than the idea itself," Billy said. "Not many people are prepared mentally and emotionally to deal with something bigger than life, and it's hard for them to absorb and see in the context of how this 'waste of time' could possibly bring positive benefits to the community."

Billy and his team persisted, steering clear of experts and consultants who only told them "it couldn't be done."

"One thing about me that remains a constant—I don't like negative people around me," he said. "We didn't need to be constantly reminded of the odds against us; we needed someone who could be positive and come up with a strategy and a solution. We ended up doing virtually everything ourselves, and we made a conscious decision to learn from our own mistakes."

With Young in the forefront, Billy and his team went abroad, taking a little taste of Atlanta with them. They set up an "Atlanta House" at each stop and invited IOC delegates to share a night of Southern cuisine and hospitality. Their goal: to make the delegates like the folks from Atlanta more than they liked the folks from anywhere else.

Billy, now as president and CEO of the Atlanta Committee for the Olympic Games (ACOG), was spending twenty days every month traveling around the world. He drew no salary or travel expenses. He just kept moving, believing that "the Olympics is an idea founded in goodness, and its goodness would make it achievable."

Weeks stretched into months, and months into two and a half years. Then it was finally time for the IOC to make its decision. In the middle of a meeting, the night before the vote, Billy's chest felt like it had exploded. "I walked toward my friend Charlie Battle, an associate, and said 'Get me out of here.' I walked out with a smile on my face, but he was literally supporting my weight," Billy said. "I was terrified but couldn't show it."

Local doctors examined Billy and decided it wasn't his heart this time, it was stress. Even then, Billy and his team didn't want others to find out about his condition, fearing it might negatively impact the vote. The next day, September 18, 1990, Billy and his team's southern hospitality paid off. Defying all tradition and conventional politics, the IOC chose Atlanta to host the 1996 Olympic Games.

"It was one of the great moments of my life," Billy reminisced. "You're prepared for the worst and hoping for the best. The feeling is indescribable."

Back home, Atlanta celebrated. A billboard went up with the slogan, "No Payne/No Gain! Thank You Billy!" But Billy knew his work had just begun. He and his team would need five full years to orchestrate an intricately detailed campaign to coordinate and fund the games. This time, Billy at least had a salary, but his job was to raise $1.5 billion through corporate sponsorships and private-sector sources. Again, everyone said the goal was impossible. And again, Billy turned to his friends.

"It took longer than we thought," Billy admitted. "If Nations Bank hadn't stepped in with a $300 million letter of credit, we could have had some problems. We had no evidence we could pay the money back, but it was a statement of faith and confidence that ultimately leveraged others to give us their support."

Billy and the ACOG went back to the Chamber of Commerce, the same group that had been polite in its rejection one year prior, and this time they raised $5.5 million in less than a week and a half. Sponsorships added up to an unprecedented $40 million. And when the ACOG asked for $400 million for U.S. television rights, the experts thought it was impossible because NBC had lost $100 million in the 1992 Olympics in Barcelona. In the end, Billy and his team got $456 million for television rights.

But success came with a personal price. To ensure that his dream became a reality, Billy started work at 4:00 A.M. each morning and continued late into the night. He exerted every ounce of energy, working until he was physically exhausted, then picking up the next morning and starting again. The rigorous demands became too much for his heart; this time, Billy found himself back in the hospital, facing triple bypass surgery. Billy's friends, understandably shaken, kept the Olympic effort moving while he recuperated. Within a month, against doctors' orders, Billy was back on the job.

Billy eventually raised every dollar needed to honor his promise and host the Olympics.

After nine long years of hard work and enormous commitment, Billy accomplished what nearly everyone had said could not be done. An estimated 5 million people from around the world gathered together for seventeen unforgettable days and participated in a piece of history that began 2,500 years ago. And Billy Payne was there relishing every moment from the opening ceremonies to the closing ceremonies, surrounded by the people who had helped him make it happen. His team. His partners. His friends.

■ **"For an endeavor anywhere near this magnitude, your success depends on the capacity of other people to carry it successfully to the end. There are no Lone Rangers. My individual effect on the outcome probably ended five years ago. As other individuals, through empowerment, took on significant responsibilities with zealous commitment, we all enjoyed success."**

—Billy Payne

·unstoppable·

"People need role models
at every stage of their lives...
not just when they're kids.
Don't expect a role model
to come along all by him or herself.
There are plenty of classy people
out there who want to help.
Instead of waiting for somebody
to take you under their wing,
go out there and find a good wing
to climb under."

—Dave Thomas,
Founder of Wendy's Old Fashioned Hamburgers

▪ In Their Own Words ▪

"After eight years of sixty grueling *marathon swim competitions across many of the world's most imposing lakes and oceans, I imagined finishing my athletic career with an unfathomable adventure. At the time, the open-water record for both men and women was sixty miles, and I dreamed of stroking one hundred nonstop miles in the ocean. After weeks of research, I chose the route between the islands of the Bahamas and the Florida coast. This would take two full days of hard-paced swimming, and it was obvious to me that I could not accomplish this alone.*

"The standard races on the marathon swim circuit are from twenty-five to forty miles, and for those distances you rely on one intimate, a coach or trainer, who stays about ten meters from you in a small boat, providing you with nourishment, encouragement, and information on where you stand in the race.

"Swimming one hundred miles in the open sea is a far more complex undertaking. Issues such as navigating rough waters, calculating changing wind currents, looking out for sharks, and maintaining glycogen levels become crucial to reaching the other shore. I knew success would require a sophisticated team.

"My job was to train some eight hours a day for a year. During that time, I assembled a team that had expertise—not to mention a grand sense of adventure and friendship—in several areas. I asked longtime America's Cup navigation expert Ken Gundersen to guide me across. Ken not only chose the optimal moment to begin but literally changed our course every fifteen minutes as winds and currents and obstacles crossed our path. Ken also brought with him a crew of young men to keep our flotilla of boats operating on course for two straight days at a near idle of two miles per hour.

"Jacques Cousteau kindly provided four expert divers familiar with sharks. Using sonar, they identified large bodies under me and dived

down to distract them. I had also sought advice from NASA's endurance specialist to efficiently keep up my glycogen level and he suggested a feeding every hour of 1,100 calories of pure glucose. In training, the sweetness of the glucose mixed with the salty sea made me nauseous, so he helped me experiment with adding plain yogurt to cut the sweetness.

"Marathon swimming is similar to boxing in that your corner men, the personal trainers in my case, psych you back up when you are disoriented or down. I lost twenty-nine pounds on my Bahamas swim, and with that duress came uncontrollable shivers, nausea, hallucinations, and even despair. Just when I felt that I couldn't go on, one of my trainers, close friends all, would say just the right words to get me to take just twenty more strokes. After that, I felt if I could make another twenty, I could make another fifty, and if I could make fifty, I could make one hundred.

"That world record of 102.5 miles, for both men and women, remains unbeaten to this day. It is mine in the record books, but there are fifty-one people, my team, who know how valuable their efforts were to my success. We all need someone in life's great marathon to buoy us and believe in us when the inevitable waves of defeat try to knock us down."

Diana Nyad

For a decade, Diana Nyad was the world's greatest long distance swimmer. She set the world record for the longest swim in history, 102.5 miles, and is considered one of the pioneers of women's sports.

▪ In Their Own Words ▪

"At thirty-five, I found myself divorced, *unemployed, and concerned about how I would support my two children. In the past, I worked part time in my husband's crane and truck rental company. Now I was faced with what to do next. Being somewhat familiar with the construction industry, I decided to start my own company specializing in erecting and installing heavy industrial equipment.*

"People weren't even polite when I told them of my plans. They said I was out of my mind to attempt this, that I had too little experience, and the economy in Denver was going downhill, just for starters. I didn't have a Plan B so this had to work, and I forged ahead.

"I took my $50,000 in savings, rented a small building, and purchased a thirteen-year-old truck. I knew I had gaping holes of knowledge, and if this had any chance of working, I needed to develop a team that would fill those holes. To do so, I sought people who had an intimate working knowledge of the construction industry.

"The first thing I did was hire field personnel with strong technical skills. Then I found a bonding and insurance company through a friend of mine in the construction industry. He introduced me to a bank familiar with construction lending. We added an attorney and a CPA, both of whom had extensive experience in the construction industry. Fifteen years later, all of those people are still with me, my unofficial board of directors.

"I have been successful because I honestly assessed my strengths and weaknesses and built a team of people who had the expertise I needed to help me take my company where I wanted it to go."

Barbara Grogan is president of Western Industrial Contractors, a Denver construction and consulting firm she started in 1982 that has grown into a $10 million business.

YOUR PERSONAL ACTION PLAN

Building Your Team

"When spider webs unite, they can tie up a lion."

—Ethiopian proverb

Behind every great achiever is another achiever. No one attains greatness by themselves. Once you've committed yourself to becoming unstoppable, you can begin to draw on the vast number of people and resources that can help you. Other unstoppable people are your greatest resource of all. All you need to do is seek them out and ask for help. They will seldom refuse.

Pole vaulter and two-time Olympic gold medalist, Bob Richards, told of the time he was working to break Dutch Warmerdam's record. No matter how he tried, he was still a foot below that record. Finally, in a bold move, he picked up the phone and called Dutch himself and asked for help. Dutch invited him for a visit, promising to give him all he had. And he did. He spent three days coaching Bob and correcting his mistakes. As a result, Bob's performance went up by eight inches.

Unstoppable people are willing to help others become unstoppable. When Gertrude Boyle saw her clothing company was in trouble, she went to an executive at Nike who willingly gave her advice. When Craig Kielburger sought the support of classmates, union members, and government leaders to work with him toward the elimination of the exploitation of children, they freely gave their assistance. And when Diana Nyad committed herself to setting a new world record of swimming one hundred nonstop miles in the ocean, she found a team of people who not only had the expertise but also shared her sense of adventure.

Step 1: Identify Role Models for Strength and Inspiration

The people in *Unstoppable* were inspired by all sorts of individuals: great leaders from the past, people who achieved excellence in a particular field, even fictional and mythological characters. Inspirational role models demonstrate what's possible and provide an invaluable source for motivation, strength, and hope.

Many people found their first role models in characters in books, and these characters became examples for them their entire lives. This source of inspiration was certainly the case with talk show host Oprah Winfrey. Oprah read about heroes and heroines as a child and internalized these fictional role models. She later said that these heroic figures provided the "open door" in her life. They gave her hope and a new realization of her own potential.

Arnold Schwarzenegger found his role model, Reg Park, in a bodybuilding magazine. Reg was the most powerful person in bodybuilding at that time, and Arnold dreamed of having huge muscles like Reg's. Arnold learned everything he could about Reg—his training routine, diet, and lifestyle. The more he learned about Reg and followed his example, the more Arnold realized it was possible for him to become like Reg.

Others have found their role models in video and audio cassettes, as Pam Lontos did with her motivational tapes. For Stephen Cannell, it was his own father. Role models are everywhere, in many forms.

This book features forty-five people who can serve as role models for you. Draw strength from those who most inspire you. These people are inarguable proof of what's possible if you refuse to be stopped.

Action: Create your own Gallery of Unstoppable Role Models. This concept was provided by Christopher Hegarty, author and speaker, and a dear friend. In his twenty years of offering seminars, his participants agree that this idea greatly impacted their lives. You might want to try it as well.

To create your gallery, first identify three or four individuals who truly inspire you. Perhaps their dreams closely resemble your own. Maybe it was the types of obstacles they faced with which you can most identify. Learn as much as you can about what kept them going when times grew tough and *how* they overcame those challenges and achieved their goals.

Find pictures of these people and hang the pictures in a place where you spend quiet time for reflection. If you don't have such a place, put the pictures in your office or any other place where you will see them frequently.

When facing a challenging situation or feeling discouraged, look at the pictures of your role models. Draw strength from their spirit. Remind yourself that they have been where you are and that they prevailed. If they prevailed, so can you!

While I was writing this book, my spirit was renewed

countless times by reflecting on the lives of the people featured in this book. At times when cash flow was nonexistent, I thought of Tom Monaghan, founder of Domino's Pizza (you'll meet him in chapter 7). Tom suffered devastating financial setbacks for *years* and yet he never gave up. When someone didn't share my enthusiasm for a particular idea because "it had never done been done before," I thought of Billy Payne and his Olympic dream. Nearly everyone told him his dream was impossible, yet he made it happen! During moments of doubt when I questioned if my goals were perhaps too "big" or "unreachable," I drew strength from Pam Lontos, who achieved unprecedented results because she didn't know it wasn't possible. Because they prevailed, I believed I too would prevail.

■ **"The capacity for hope is the most significant fact of life. It gives human beings a sense of destination and the energy to get started."**

—Norman Cousins

Step 2: Inventory Your Existing Contacts

You're Only a Phone Call Away from ANYONE

Billy Payne's story clearly demonstrates the power of friends to help turn your dream into a reality. You may argue that you don't have friends as influential as Billy Payne's. However, your network is undoubtedly more extensive than you realize. Your actual network extends well beyond your day-to-day contacts. This larger network includes the people you work with and have worked with in the past, former classmates and alumni, friends, members of your extended family, people at the church or synagogue you attend, the local Chamber of Commerce, parents you've met from your child's school, and people you've met at seminars or conventions. Your network also includes everyone the people in the network know and have contacts with.

There's a saying that anyone is only six people from the president. You know someone who knows someone who knows someone...right up to the Oval Office. And if you're only six people away from the president, you're only six people away from anyone you want to meet, whether it's a corporate CEO, a Hollywood producer, or a celebrity whose help you'd like to enlist to support a cause.

Draw on Your Existing Relationships

People like doing business with people they like, and they also like helping people they like. When I started this book, I knew that if I wanted to achieve my goals, I would need to align myself with top-notch individuals who had a track record of packaging, distributing, and marketing best-selling books. As an unknown author, people weren't exactly beating down my door to work with me.

A key sales strategy for pitching an idea to someone when you or your product is unknown is to associate it with other well-known people. Or, as Harvey Mackay says, "If you don't have a big name, borrow one." The most widely recognized person I knew at the time was Paul Orfalea, the chairperson and founder of Kinko's, Inc. Kinko's had been my customer for more than six years when I worked at Sprint. I had worked diligently for Kinko's and had a good business relationship with Paul. After leaving Sprint, I asked Paul on several occasions to write letters on my behalf. He generously agreed. Those letters of endorsement from Paul gave credibility to my project and positioned me in a different light than if I had sent out my book without Paul's letter.

Action: Make a list of all of your contacts. Think of everyone you know and have done business with right up to the CEO of a company that has been a past client. Design a strategy that best uses your contacts. Maybe you'd like someone to make a phone call on your behalf, refer you to a contact in a particular industry, or write a letter of endorsement. By all means, make it easy for people to help you. If you're asking for a letter, draft it for them. The draft will save them a great deal of time since they won't have to create it from scratch. When you send the draft, also send them your FedEx account number or a self-addressed stamped envelope. Most people are willing to help. They haven't achieved prominent positions by being passive, and of all people, powerful people respect a little "chutzpah" when they see it in others. Don't be afraid to ask. By not asking, you are saying no for them.

STEP 3: DEVELOP YOUR OWN "INNER CIRCLE"

You don't have to come from corporate America to be aware of the term the "old boy's club." This elite "club" can be found in every field. Unfortunately, most of us aren't members. For decades, men in senior executive positions have been masters at effectively building their teams. The result of their efforts has been a strong support system that benefits every area of their lives.

These relationships did not magically happen. The relationships were developed over years of invested time and energy. They golfed with colleagues and business associates, participated in community fund-raisers, and joined country clubs and business organizations.

Networking is a skill that is never taught in school but is absolutely crucial if your dream requires the support of others. Why not follow the examples of those who do it best? In my opinion, Harvey Mackay is one of the all-time masters of networking. His book, *Dig Your Well Before You're Thirsty* is an excellent resource for providing you with additional insights on how to build and maintain your own personal network.

Your goal may not be to become a senior officer in a corporation—it doesn't matter. Whatever your goal is, the principles are the same. Everyone can benefit from their own inner circle.

> ■ **"From the beginning of time, those who became leaders were not necessarily the strongest or fiercest...but those with the most friends or connections."**
>
> —*William F. Allman, Author,* **The Stone Age Present**

Find Candidates for Your "Inner Circle"

- **Nonprofit organizations:** The absolute best place to find caring, action-oriented people is at nonprofit organizations. The boards of directors of most nonprofits comprise corporate executives, entrepreneurs, and community leaders. No matter how busy you may be, if you're not involved in a nonprofit, you are missing a great opportunity to invest in people. At the same time, you'll be working alongside the movers and shakers in your community.

  Identify a nonprofit that compliments your purpose and passion. Volunteer for a committee. By giving of your time and resources, you'll gain the opportunity to make a difference in your community and meet great people you might not have ordinarily come in contact with.

- **Professional associations and conventions:** People gather from all over the country to share ideas, methods, and techniques at industry conventions. These meetings offer an excellent forum to make new connections and personally meet top achievers in almost any field. Do your research. After identifying the industry or field you want to pursue, go to the library or go on-line with your computer and look up the associations listed under that category. Call the association and request an information kit along with a list of upcoming conventions, seminars, and available publications and other materials. Identify the people you most want to meet, attend the meetings, and introduce yourself. Don't be shy!

- **Your existing place of employment:** If you are currently working for a corporation, don't miss a valuable opportunity to maximize your existing resources. Every employee has a title and a job description. Unfortunately, many employees refuse to do anything outside of their job description. If you want to grow and become unstoppable, you must step "out of the box" and move beyond the confines of your job description. Be proactive. Many employers offer unprecedented opportunities to anyone who is assertive and creative. Some people have told me that I've developed this concept to a "fine art."

  As an example, while working for Sprint, I sold a $30 million contract that included the first-ever national retail videoconferencing network. An account of this scope required the support of numerous divisions within the company. Instead of staying within my job description—national account manager (sales)—I actively got involved in all aspects of the account, including project management, implementation, training, marketing, and public relations. A typical national account manager might participate in many of those meetings, but I took it the next step. Here are just two examples:

In one instance, my customer, Kinko's, Inc., was having a national sales conference. Kinko's requested that a Sprint executive present a keynote address to its 750 salespeople on Sprint and Kinko's new videoconferencing partnership. I volunteered. *I'm sure Kinko's was envisioning someone a little higher in the food chain than its sales rep!* I, however, viewed the speech as a great opportunity to stretch myself and take my presentation skills to the next level. After consideration, Kinko's accepted my offer.

Because I had never before spoken to a group that size, I wanted to be as prepared as possible. I joined the National Speakers Association, attended speaking workshops, and hired a professional speaker and magician to participate in the meeting. Now, I wasn't exactly Tony Robbins, but the presentation went well and I gained invaluable experience in speaking to a large audience. A few months later, Kinko's wanted a Sprint representative to speak at its annual company meeting with 2,500 in attendance. This time they called me.

In another instance, Sprint had the task of cost-effectively training 750 sales reps in over 150 locations nationwide on how to sell videoconferencing. Again, I volunteered. I wasn't a trainer, but who better to train salespeople about selling a product than another salesperson? With the support of Sprint's and Kinko's training department, we designed a videoconferencing road show. I, along with two other people, trained salespeople in 150 locations in less than eight weeks using the videoconferencing technology. We didn't have to pack one suitcase. In doing this project, I learned and expanded my skills and experience.

I could have easily handed both of these opportunities to the "appropriate" departments. These projects were clearly outside of my job description and were a little intimidating since I had never done anything like either of them before. But because I boldly seized the opportunity, I unknowingly set in motion a new direction for my career—public speaking—that I hadn't originally explored.

Think of opportunities that you could develop more fully. How could you maximize the job you currently have? What special projects could you volunteer to lead? Whom do you admire in your company and want to learn from? Step outside the "box." No one will create these opportunities for you. You have to do it. In doing so, you'll benefit from working with people you might not have originally had the opportunity to work with; in the process, you will expand your abilities and expose yourself to options you never before considered.

- **Find a coach:** Personal coaches are becoming a unique profession of the 1990s. Coaches work with all types of individuals to help define and achieve goals: career, personal, or most often both. Coaches' fees generally range from $150 to $500 a month for weekly half-hour telephone sessions. A coach might consult on everything from starting a business to improving your backhand in tennis.

  If coaching fees do not fit within your budget, there is an alternative. Find an individual who has expertise in an area where you require support. Think about the skills and abilities you have that could be useful to that person and then trade time coaching each other.

  To illustrate this concept, I met a wonderful person on a flight from Nashville who has since become a dear friend. He is an independent promotions manager for several major record labels and has worked for some of the top recording artists. He has twenty years of experience in the industry and has developed promotions for artists that have resulted in the sales of over 1 billion records. I briefly told him about my plans for my book, and he shared with me some of his all-time most successful and outrageous promotions.

As we continued to talk, I discovered his goal was to become a marketing executive with a major record label. As an outsider, I was able to see that he had many marketable skills and a consistent track record that he took for granted and needed to leverage more fully. Drawing from my corporate experience and the strategies I had used in my own business, I was able to share possible positioning strategies that he hadn't considered. We keep in touch regularly through email and share suggestions on how we can each achieve our objectives. We both benefit from each other's expertise and, more importantly, encouragement. And the price is right!

Action: Identify an area where you would like to learn more. You may have plans to start a consulting business, to become a recording artist, or to develop a new product for the Internet. Who could provide the needed expertise? List as many potential resources as possible. If it is someone in your company, approach that person. Talk to your inner circle, and ask them if they know anyone in that field. Usually, each name you get will result in another referral until you meet the person you need to meet. If all of your leads eventually become dead-ends, do some research. Identify those who have written recent articles about the subject. Write each of them a letter with your questions or use email, which now provides swift and easy access to all sorts of individuals from college professors to corporate presidents. Ask these people for possible referrals or suggestions for other resources. Even

Bill Gates can be reached by email. Take advantage of technology, and most important, take action! You have nothing to lose, and each step will bring you closer to your goal.

■ **"A wise man learns by the experience of others. An ordinary man learns by his own experience. A fool learns by nobody's experience."**

—Vern McLellan

Step 4: Develop a Mastermind Group—Your Personal Advisory Board

In his book *Think and Grow Rich*, Napoleon Hill defines a mastermind group as the "coordination of knowledge and effort, in a spirit of harmony between two or more people, for the attainment of a definite purpose." If "two heads are better than one," when you have an entire team, you have exponential magic. Hill goes on to say that "economic advantages may be created by any person who surrounds themselves with the advice, counsel, and personal cooperation of a group who are willing to lend him or her wholehearted aid in a spirit of harmony. This form of cooperative alliance has been the basis of nearly every great fortune." Translation: Two heads are more successful than one.

Sherry Phelan, speaker, facilitator, and founder of TAP Turn-Around Programs, has led mastermind groups for all kinds of individuals and organizations. She sees three main benefits to these groups: they serve as (1) a sounding board, (2) an information and resource board, and (3) an accountability board.

You can benefit from a mastermind group whether your dream is to sail around the world, write a script, or support a cause.

Many people have similar interests or skills that can help you and who can be helped by your expertise. Members of a mastermind group bring together their varied backgrounds, information, and contacts for one specific reason: to help each group member achieve his or her goals.

A mastermind group provides a great opportunity to allow your inner circle to benefit others. Each of you has contacts and knowledge that can be of value to a variety of people whether he or she works for a nonprofit organization or is an executive with a Fortune 500 company. Here's a personal example that I would have never anticipated. When I was interviewing Kemmons Wilson, founder of Holiday Inns, for this book, he read in my biography that I had sold a videoconferencing contract to Kinko's. He was interested in researching the viability of placing videoconferencing centers at Holiday Inns worldwide. I was able to give him suggestions on how to pursue this opportunity and put him in touch with people with whom he could possibly form an alliance. It would have never occurred to me that I could be a valuable resource to this famous innovator.

Finally, don't underestimate who and what you know. Always look for ways you can offer help first. Build a reputation for being a "giver." Brainstorm how your expertise or contacts can help others. If people dash out of your path or hide in stairwells when you walk down the hall, you might need to reconsider your approach.

Be the first to give. You'll derive personal satisfaction in helping others. And remember the law of the universe, "What goes around, comes around." If you focus on giving and being of service to others, people will want to give back to you!

Action: Identify three areas where you require support. Identify one person this week who could provide support in one of those areas and invite that person to join your mastermind group. Brainstorm with that person about how you could help each other achieve your respective goals. Discuss possible future members for the mastermind group, existing contacts, and resources you might each have that would help one another. Offer to set up introductions for one another.

When it comes to teamwork, the math you learned in school doesn't apply. One plus one equals far more than two. And one plus any other number can equal unstoppable results.

(Note: For more information about developing your own mastermind group, see the Appendix.)

•Characteristic Six•

CREATIVITY
Taps Unconscious Resources

It's happened to everyone who has a goal. You decide what you want, develop a plan, take the first step, and then the unexpected happens.

The loan falls through. Your partner decides to give it all up and move to the country. You see an ad for the same product you've been developing for three years.

Things *never* work out exactly as intended, and the six people you're about to meet in this chapter can certainly vouch for that. Creativity played a key role in allowing them to conquer daily battles. If they hadn't come up with alternative solutions, their dreams would have died, and the obstacles would have triumphed.

"Your Personal Action Plan" will provide you with ways to rejuvenate your dream by expanding your inborn creativity and identifying new approaches to solve any problem. Unstoppable people believe there's always a solution. When you share that belief, you are already halfway to your goal!

■ **"Obstacles don't have to stop you. If you run into a wall, don't turn around and give up. Figure out how to climb it, go through it, or work around it."**

—Michael Jordan

Putting a New Face on Business

The Creation of a Caring Corporation

If you want to start a successful business:

- Don't choose an industry that's already dominated by several large companies.
- Don't plan on selling products without an advertising campaign.
- Don't mix politics with sales.

Any Harvard Business School graduate can tell you those rules. And that's exactly why someone from Harvard Business School is the last person Anita Roddick plans to hire.

Anita broke just about every rule in the book when she started The Body Shop to sell naturally-based cosmetics. She's still breaking the rules today. Of course, such irreverence has its consequences. In Anita's case, the consequences read like this: The Body Shop now has more than 1,500 stores throughout the world, is worth over $500 million, and has influenced the products and marketing of all its chief competitors. And those are just the consequences in the business arena. The Body Shop is also a powerfully effective vehicle for social and environmental awareness and change; as far as Anita is concerned, that is the most important consequence of all.

From the moment in 1976 when Anita first conceived the idea of opening a shop to sell naturally-based cosmetics, she was thinking in a most unbusinesslike manner. Most entrepreneurs set out to establish a company with growth potential that will make them wealthy someday. Anita was just looking for a way to feed herself and her two children, while her husband, also a maverick, was away on a two-year adventure, riding a horse from Argentina to New York.

Her first challenge was to find a cosmetics manufacturer to produce her products. No one she approached had ever heard of jojoba oil or aloe vera gel, and they all thought that cocoa butter had something to do with chocolate. Although she didn't realize it at the time, Anita had discovered a market just about to explode: young female consumers who would prefer their cosmetics to be produced in a cruelty-free and environmentally responsible manner. When manufacturers failed to have the same foresight, Anita found a small herbalist who could do the work she required.

Since Anita was not the typical entrepreneur, she saw no drawbacks in starting her company with almost no capital. To save money, she bottled her cosmetics in the same inexpensive plastic containers hospitals use for urine samples, encouraging her customers to bring the containers back for refills. Because Anita couldn't afford to have labels printed, she and some friends hand printed every one. Her packaging couldn't have turned out better if she'd planned it that way. With the improvised packaging, her product now had the same natural, earthy image as the cosmetics themselves.

Anita opened the first branch of The Body Shop in Brighton, England. When she first opened, neighboring proprietors made bets on how long the store would last. Less amused were the owners of local funeral parlors who insisted she change the shop's name. No one, they complained, would hire a funeral director located near a place called "The Body Shop." She stuck to her guns and the name stayed.

The first store was only minimally successful. Nevertheless, Anita decided to move ahead with a second one. The bank questioned the wisdom of her plan and refused a loan. So she found a friend of a friend who was willing to lend her the equivalent of $6,400 in exchange for 50 percent ownership of The Body Shop. Today that person is worth $140 million. Signing over half of her business was the only real mistake Anita ever made. But it wasn't the only decision that looked like a mistake. Here are three more:

- She has never advertised even when she opened shops in the United States. People told her it was suicide to enter a new market without massive advertising support.
- She doesn't sell in any outlet other than The Body Shop stores. (Some of her Asian stores are the only exception and are located within department stores.)
- She resolved early on that her shops would be a catalyst for change, not just in the business world, but in the world at large.

These decisions turned out to be some of the most inspired "mistakes" in the history of retailing. Even though up until the mid-'90s Anita had never paid for advertising, her unconventional ideas have inspired hundreds of articles and interviews generating tremendous publicity. Her first shop in New York was packed with customers from the day it opened. At one point, a thirty-five-year-old woman on roller skates threw up her arms and shouted, "Hallelujah! You're here at last." So much for advertising.

A new branch of The Body Shop opens somewhere in the world every two and a half days. Occasionally, Anita has had trouble opening stores in shopping malls. But having a past that was filled with challenges, Anita is accustomed to coming up with creative solutions. For instance, when one mall refused to lease her space, she organized every mail-order customer within a 110-mile radius to write letters to the management of that mall. Within a few months, a branch of The Body Shop was open.

Anita also had this nonconformist idea of putting ideals ahead of profit. From the start, Anita wanted not just to change the faces of her customers but to change the entire face of business. She envisioned a company that was socially responsible and compassionate. "I see the human spirit playing a big role in business. The work does not have to be drudgery, and the sole focus does not have to be on making money. It can be a human enterprise that people feel genuinely good about."

Some of the raw materials for her products are harvested by groups of people in underdeveloped regions, thus generating an income for them. The Body Shop has launched campaigns to save the whales, ban animal testing in the cosmetics industry, help the homeless, and protect the rain forests. All of these campaigns have been eagerly supported by loyal customers.

Employees of The Body Shop are actively involved in these efforts. Each month, employees receive a half day off with pay to volunteer in the community. Some employees, for example, went to Romania to help rebuild orphanages. In the stores, customers are encouraged to register to vote, recycle their plastic cosmetics containers, and bring their own shopping bags to save paper and plastic. Because of all these activities, people have suggested

Anita's company should really be called "The Body and Soul Shop." Customers emerge not only looking good but also feeling good.

"Business as usual" isn't part of Anita Roddick's make up. But as far as she's concerned, doing what is not usual has made all the difference.

■ **"What saved us over and over was our willingness to recognize what wasn't working and quickly identify a new way of looking at it. By remaining flexible and open to creative solutions, the results have been miraculous."**

—Anita Roddick

▪ Something to Think About ▪

Stephen Hilbert, president and CEO of Conseco, Inc., said that raising money for Conseco was the hardest job of his life. He could not find a single investor or bank willing to invest in his start-up insurance company.

Instead of giving up, he and his partner hit the streets. Stephen had sold encyclopedias door-to-door part time during college and came up with the idea to sell shares in his company the same way. Keep in mind that this was in 1980 when people could invest in a money market account and earn 17 percent interest.

Stephen and his partner asked individuals to buy shares in their start-up company from a three-page business plan. Between 1979 and 1982, they knocked on thousands of doors and ultimately raised close to $4 million.

Conseco is now a billion dollar insurance company and Stephen Hilbert, at the age of 51, made *Forbes's* 1997 list of the 400 Richest People in the World.

UNSTOPPABLE
GEORGE CRENSHAW

▪ UNSTOPPABLE ▪

How to Rescue a Neighborhood

Creativity Was Rocky's Theme

His name is James, but people call him Rocky. The name fits. He's big, over six feet tall, and he's tough when he needs to be. James "Rocky" Robinson lives and works in New York City's Bedford-Stuyvesant district, one of the most impoverished and dangerous neighborhoods in the United States. Yet it is here in "Bed-Stuy" that he is saving lives and reviving a community like no one has before.

In 1966, when Rocky was twenty-six years old, his seven-year-old niece was struck by a car on the streets of Bed-Stuy. Had someone at the scene known first aid or CPR, she might have lived. But by the time she reached a hospital, she was dead.

His niece's unnecessary death was one reason Rocky became a paramedic. Working for the Emergency Medical Service of New York City, he realized that more than half the city's emergency calls came from high-crime areas. According to Rocky, residents of crime-plagued minority neighborhoods like Bed-Stuy sometimes had to wait as long as 26 minutes after calling 911 for an ambulance; calls in more affluent white communities were answered in a fraction of the time. Too many people died who didn't have to—people like Rocky's young niece, because they had to wait for an ambulance.

Rocky decided to find out more about the problem. His research revealed that the more affluent communities had organized their own ambulance corps to supplement city services because the city was overwhelmed with calls. "If that's the key to success," he told his friend and EMT (emergency medical technician) colleague, Joe Perez, "we'll start our own corps in Bed-Stuy!"

In 1988, Rocky had no idea that he and Joe would be attempting to establish the first minority-run ambulance service in the country, or just how creative he would have to be to overcome the obstacles. The pair's first challenge was to find a location for the headquarters. They took over an abandoned building that was commonly used by drug dealers. "If junkies could use it to take lives, we could darn well use it to save lives," said Rocky. Because there was no electricity or running water (except for the leaks in the roof) the two men worked during daylight hours. They used a two-way radio to receive emergency calls.

Although they could make do with their new headquarters, Rocky and Joe still lacked the most important component of an ambulance service: an ambulance. An old Chevrolet got them to the scenes of accidents, fires, shootings, and stabbings. But the car didn't always start. At times, they were forced to strap their trauma kits and oxygen tanks to their backs and run on foot to the emergencies. To save lives, they often ran past jeering drug dealers, wise-cracking cops, and astonished onlookers. Everyone laughed, except the victims who were still alive when Rocky and Joe arrived.

The drafty old building was too cold in the winter. A trailer was donated and Rocky and Joe moved the trailer to a lot across the street. They knocked down two shacks used by local drug dealers and set up shop themselves. To the drug dealers, the trailer was a call to battle. For eight months, the drug dealers tried to scare Rocky off their turf. They shot out the windows in the trailer and threatened to burn it down. They shot at Rocky and Joe when the two headed out on emergency calls. Rocky stayed low to the ground and kept going. The drug dealers didn't give up until they finally realized the two men were saving some of their own people after bouts of bloody street violence.

The two EMTs even took shots, the verbal kind, from their own colleagues, some of whom saw them as competitors. Both men became the target of cruel jokes, harassment, and rumors that they were incompetent. Rocky knew there was only one way to silence the detractors—he and Joe had to transform their shoestring operation into a full-fledged, well-trained unit that could capably answer every call and save every life possible.

To accomplish that transformation, Rocky needed a crew of volunteers, an authentic "corps." To build his corps, he drew from the community. Bed-Stuy was typical of many other inner-city communities. Within Bed-Stuy there were 250 crack houses, hundreds of drug dealers and prostitutes on the streets, a large population of homeless persons and teenage dropouts, and as many residents on welfare as blue-collar wage-earners. Many of the residents weren't convinced a fledgling volunteer corps could provide them with anything they couldn't already get by dialing 911.

So Rocky and Joe blanketed the neighborhood with flyers and explained their new service to anyone who would listen. As residents saw the duo rushing to emergencies, on foot or by car, saving their neighbors and loved ones who might otherwise have died, they began to see the light.

Rocky got his volunteers from among recovering alcoholics, the unemployed, even drug dealers trying to go straight. Within months, Rocky and Joe had drafted dozens of young people and were training them to rescue others. After receiving training in first aid and CPR, the volunteers responded to calls. In the process, many of the volunteers learned skills, found a purpose in life, and rescued themselves from despair. Some went on to become nurses and doctors. Rocky wasn't just saving the dying anymore—he was also saving the living.

Eventually, the *Daily News* ran a story about the "guys running around the neighborhood with oxygen tanks on their backs." A philanthropist read the story and donated an old ambulance to the cause. At last, Rocky had his ambulance corps. On the first day with the ambulance, the corps arrived first at the scene of a fire and rescued ten people from a burning building. The next day, they delivered a baby. Time after time, Rocky, Joe, and the volunteers were the first on the scene, and even Rocky's critics in the city's Emergency Medical Service began to see their value.

Donations and grants from foundations began to pour in. A group of people from Montana wrote, "We're a bunch of rednecks up here, but we're inspired by what you're doing and we want to help." When times were bad and funding was low, Rocky found other ways to come up with money. He sold car washes and solicited donations in the streets. He would do anything to pay the rent, train the volunteers, and buy supplies—anything to save lives.

Today, the Bedford-Stuyvesant Volunteer Ambulance Corps, the first minority-run ambulance corps in the nation, has 350 volunteers. The organization responds to 300 emergency calls a month—calls from grateful police, understaffed city emergency services, and citizens who know they can count on fast, reliable service.

It is not usually possible to calculate the value of imagination and the creative spirit, but it is in the case of Rocky Robinson and his partner, Joe Perez. The value is twenty-six minutes—the time that makes the difference between life and death in a community of abandoned buildings and abandoned souls.

■ **"I don't let obstacles get me down. I focus on how to overcome them. You can work around any obstacle by going under it if it's too high, going over it if it's too low. There's always a way!"**

—James "Rocky" Robinson

UNSTOPPABLE
GEORGE CRENSHAW

·unstoppable·

"You may have to fight a battle more than once to win it."

— *Margaret Thatcher*

UNSTOPPABLE

The Sweet Smell of Success

He Was Nutty Enough to Find New Ways Past Old Obstacles

He had it all. A cushy job as a financial analyst with a Fortune 500 company. A nice house in Hilton Head, South Carolina, one of the loveliest places in the United States. A new bride he was crazy about. So what did John Mautner do? He risked everything he had on one of the nuttiest schemes ever to come down the pike.

John was frustrated. His ultimate earning potential at his current position would never provide him the type of personal or financial freedom he was seeking, and the struggle of climbing the corporate ladder had lost its appeal. John wanted financial independence. He believed running his own business was the key to achieving that security.

But John wasn't like most people. He did more than just dream about it—he acted. In 1990, he quit his job, gave up his nice house, and left beautiful Hilton Head. With his friends and family members telling him he was crazy, he and his wife, Anne, moved to Orlando, Florida, a city with an abundant tourist trade.

John saw his route to financial independence paved with nuts—the cinnamon-and-sugar-coated kind, sold piping hot to customers on the street. Inspired by the pushcart entrepreneurs who work the sidewalks of cities in Europe and propelled by his love of cooking, John spent long hours developing his own special recipe for glazing almonds and pecans. With a loan of $10,000 and a new name, "The Nutty Bavarian," John set up business with a single cart that allowed customers to watch as the nuts were roasted and glazed.

Creative name. Creative display. Creative product. But for all his creativity, John struggled financially. Not welcoming the competition, established concessionaires kept John out of prime commercial areas. At the end of the Nutty Bavarian's first year, John was nearly broke. Anne kept them afloat by working full time as a nurse.

John's plan was not working, so the plan had to change. In order to turn around the situation, John knew he had to get a great location. In the Orlando area, the best site for selling high quality snacks was one of the state's world-class theme parks. Getting into one of the parks, however, was another story. Florida's Universal Studios told John the only way to get into the park was to put up $100,000 and supply the product. Universal Studios would manage his cart. Major companies like Orville Redenbacher and Haagen-Dazs were already doing that, but to The Nutty Bavarian, $100,000 was a lot of pecans. To compete with the big companies, John had to find a creative way around the usual channels.

He called the food service department at Universal Studios and spoke with the vice president. John told the man about his irresistible roasted almonds and pecans. The vice president asked John to submit a proposal, which John did immediately. Weeks went by without a word from the executive. John called every day for a month. He dropped off product samples and sent letters. Finally, John sent the vice president a letter stating he wouldn't stop calling until the vice president either agreed to meet with him for thirty minutes or flat out told him to get lost.

His letter worked. The vice president agreed to a meeting. Then came the real test of John's imagination. He knew this thirty-minute meeting had to be unforgettable. Knowing that the aroma of his freshly roasted almonds and pecans was irresistible, John decided he would let his product do the talking. On the big day, John hauled his roaster into the boardroom and proceeded to make a fresh batch of cinnamon-glazed pecans. The nuts churned and clicked against the sides of a copper bowl. The aroma filled the room, then seeped into the hallways. Soon, other executives were stopping in to find out what was cooking. The executives found a bowl filled with hot, steamy, freshly glazed pecans.

John served everybody. The executives' mouths watered for more. But despite John's appeal to their salivary glands, the executives wanted more time to consider his proposal. More time? Any more time and John would be looking for a part-time job just to keep nuts in the roaster. John knew it was now or never and he had an idea. "I told them that if they gave me a thirty-day trial, I would personally operate my pushcart every day for a month, twelve hours a day, and give Universal Studios 25 percent of my sales. Universal would have no risk, and I would win the opportunity to prove myself and my product." The executives agreed to his proposal.

That first month, John grossed $40,000. Sales climbed steadily, and after the second month, John signed a two-year contract with Universal. At the end of the first year, with only two carts, John's sales reached $1 million.

"I didn't know it at the time," John said, "but they had never before allowed a food vendor to come into the park from the outside, totally independent from Universal. This was an unprecedented move."

The Nutty Bavarian now licenses carts in 150 domestic locations and three foreign countries. Annual sales exceed $10 million. John's specially roasted pecans and almonds are President Clinton's favorite snack and have been served at both of his inaugurations. The Nutty Bavarian snacks have also been featured on CNN, and Bryant Gumbel and Willard Scott raved about them on NBC's *Today Show*.

John has been kind enough to share his "secret recipe" with all of us—a dash of belief, a pinch of audacity, and a roaster full of creativity.

> ■ **"All of this was possible because I didn't stop at the first or 100th no I received. If one approach didn't work, I'd try another one, and I never gave up."**
>
> ***—John Mautner***

.unstoppable.

"The truth is that the average 'bottom-of-the-ladder' person is potentially as creative as the top executive who sits in the big office. The problem is that the person on the bottom of the ladder doesn't trust his own brilliance and doesn't, therefore, believe in his own ideas."

—*Dr. Robert H. Schuller,*
TOUGH TIMES NEVER LAST, BUT TOUGH PEOPLE DO

UNSTOPPABLE

The Power of the Creative Spirit

Moving Mountains in the Appalachians

Eula Hall has no medical license, yet she spends every day caring for the sick and injured. She's had no formal training in politics or law, but she is one of the country's most effective lobbyists and fund-raisers for the poor. No degree in social work hangs on her wall, not even a high school diploma, but she is a counselor and advocate for the aged, the poor, and the abused.

If the world gave degrees in compassion, creativity, and tenacity, Eula Hall would have a Ph.D. Instead, she is a "dirt-poor country girl" who labors in the backwoods and shanties of Kentucky's Appalachian Mountains. Her work is to relieve the human suffering in her hometown, and human suffering is one area in which Eula has had plenty of first-hand experience.

Born in Pike County, Kentucky, in 1927, Eula was one of seven children, most of whom were physically challenged in some way. Eula gave birth to five children. She had no prenatal care, and all the babies were delivered at home. One was born premature and deaf; another died in infancy. Throughout her life, children around Eula have died of malnutrition and parasites; adults have died from preventable illnesses like tetanus. These deaths occurred because the community lacked a doctor, a hospital, and medical supplies and had no money to pay for even the most basic of medical services.

By her eighteenth birthday, Eula's vision was clear. She wanted to do something to help people. This eighth-grade dropout who had never taken a science class was determined to establish a medical clinic. Her job paid $50 a week. Saving diligently what little she could for the next seven years, she amassed enough to rent a small shack for $40 a month on an isolated road in an area called Mud Creek.

Eula needed to raise funds for the clinic, but a task that proved far more difficult was "raising" doctors. Appalachia is not the stuff dreams are made of for brilliant young doctors who can make more in a month than a Mud Creek resident makes in a lifetime. Even doctors who were interested were put off by the lack of decent housing. So Eula put the doctors up in her own home and fed them her good home cooking. She attracted her medical staff from a pool of foreign doctors who were required to do service in disadvantaged areas to get their green cards.

From the moment the clinic's doors opened, it was overwhelmed with needy patients. People came with an assortment of ailments ranging from smashed fingers to congested lungs. Many patients had never seen a doctor before. Most could barely afford the $5 token fee. For three years they came to Eula's clinic for medical care they desperately needed. But Eula's ability to solve problems was about to be tested like never before.

One night the clinic caught fire and burned to the ground. Her lifelong dream and a decade of labor and sacrifice was in ruins. Standing before the smoldering rubble, Eula thought of the 15,000 residents that were now her responsibility. She thought of the work, the supplies, and equipment that lay in ashes. "Those charred remains pierced my heart deeper than anything I'd ever experienced," she recalled. First she cried. Then she gathered her courage, pushed through her grief, and announced to the staff, "The building's gone, but we're here."

That night, she put her mind to work, figuring ways to rebuild. The next day she began receiving patients outside, using a picnic bench and a telephone she persuaded the phone company to hook up to a tree. Lines formed in the field, and the staff treated patients. Eula worked to raise money in every way imaginable—by going on the radio, organizing chicken dumpling dinners, even standing on the nearest highway with a donation bucket on the days she knew people had received Social Security or disability checks. Within three months, she had raised $102,000, enough to secure a federal grant for a new clinic.

When a local school closed for the summer, Eula moved the clinic there. In the fall, she moved the clinic into a trailer. One step at a time, one dollar at a time, a new clinic rose. A modern one, with central heat and air conditioning and a paved parking lot. Because of Eula's unflagging creative vision, the flames that destroyed the original clinic had cleared the way for something bigger and better.

Today, Mud Creek Clinic stands as the only pay-what-you-can treatment center for hundreds of miles. People journey across the mountains to have their children inoculated, to have their blood pressure checked, or to get a prescription for heart medicine. If the clinic can't help them, Eula finds someone who can. She has arranged surgery for impoverished cancer patients; on one occasion, she persuaded the Lions Club to pay for corrective surgery on a little girl with badly crossed eyes. She works when necessary as the clinic's ambulance driver, racing critical patients on a two-hour drive to the nearest hospital. Once the car rolled over and she broke her shoulder. She was back at work the next morning. Her philosophy, as much as her energy, keeps her going. "We weren't promised a bed of roses," she said, "and the sun always shines after the rain."

She claims that if only she had gotten a good education, she could have done so much more for her people. It's hard to imagine what "so much more" could be. Eula has gone to court to win disability claims for the impoverished, including victims of black lung disease. She received a state grant to reorganize the water district and build a water plant to replace hundreds of contaminated wells. She raised money for a car to deliver meals to the homebound, supply free school lunches, and build a senior citizens' center. Whatever she envisioned, she turned into a reality.

Today, her phone rings without pause all day long. She herself suffers from arthritis and heart disease, but in spite of being hospitalized a few years ago, she proclaims "hard work don't kill people."

The clinic stands as a monument to Eula's powerful vision, unrelenting hard work, and creative spirit. Every day, a hundred people walk and drive the remote winding road to reach the clinic's doorstep. Inside, a staff of seventeen, including two doctors, rushes around to help patients in seven well-equipped examining rooms.

Eula lives on an annual salary of $22,000 and hasn't taken a vacation in four years. She's at the clinic every day that it is open, often until long after dark, waiting for the last patient to be examined and treated before she locks up. Only then, assured that her "children" are safe and cared for, does Eula Hall go home to rest.

■ **"Things don't just happen. You have to make them happen and you can count on nothing working out exactly as planned. By working hard and creatively looking for solutions, you will find your way around all of life's obstacles."**

—Eula Hall

▪ Something to Think About ▪

When you're up against a wall, with no apparent way around it, John Johnson, founder of *Negro Digest, Jet* magazine, and *Ebony* magazine, suggests asking yourself the following question:

"What can I do, with what I have, to get what I want?"

John's asked himself that question many times and the results have been amazing. Despite the fact that everyone told John Johnson that starting a paper for blacks about blacks was a crazy idea, he wouldn't listen. Using his mother's furniture as collateral, he borrowed $500 from a bank and on November 1, 1942, printed the first issue of *Negro Digest*.

Johnson printed 2,000 copies and was turned down by every distributor he approached. Not to be defeated, he asked thirty of his friends to drive around the city, stop at every newsstand, and ask to buy a copy of *Negro Digest*. Before long, a distributor called him and agreed to distribute the publication.

▪ In Their Own Words ▪

***"I was 22 and an accounting** student at the University of Southern California. After two semesters, I realized I didn't want to make my living as an accountant but as an entrepreneur, and I wanted to attend the highly regarded entrepreneurial program at USC's Business School.*

"The problem was I couldn't get in. The dean's office informed me that my grade point average from the previous college I attended wasn't high enough, and besides that, there were no more openings.

"I really wanted to graduate from the business school. So with all the official routes closed to me, I had to be creative and find a less obvious or less traditional path. After some thought, I came up with a strategy: I signed up for every class in the entrepreneurial program by 'crashing' each course. Crashing a course involves showing up the first day of class, even though you're not registered, then grabbing one of the slots that are created by students who over the next few weeks decide to drop out.

"In two years, I crashed all seven required courses in the entrepreneurial program and earned class credit in each. During the final semester, I went in to see the dean. I showed him my transcripts, explained how I pulled it off, and asked if I could graduate with the program, even though I wasn't technically enrolled. He was surprised—but impressed.

"'It appears to me that you're an entrepreneur in every sense of the word,' he said. 'I don't see how I can possibly deny your request.'

"That spring, I graduated from USC's Business School with a certification in its entrepreneurial program. All because I used my imagination to find a way around an obstacle I refused to let hold me back."

Tim Bearer, a successful business executive, looks back on a moment of youthful creativity and chutzpah that changed the direction of his education and his life.

▪ In Their Own Words ▪

***"When the Atlanta airport was** under construction in 1979, we were a new company struggling to make it. National Car Rental needed four acres of dirt paved so the cars could be on site when the airport opened, and the official opening was only ten days away! No other local paving company wanted to do the job, stating it couldn't be done in the short time required.*

"Because we were new and really needed the work, we were willing to try harder. We gave National a bid and promised our best effort to get the job finished within ten days. We also reminded them that if we failed, they would be no worse off, but they had plenty to gain if we succeeded.

"We were awarded the job and immediately went into action. Working double shifts required lights at night, so I rented portable generators. Our next challenge was to keep the rock mixture at the right moisture level. All the available water wagons were rented out for the airport construction, and we certainly couldn't afford to buy a new one. As an alternative, I got a special permit to rent fire engine hoses and hook up to nearby hydrants; then I personally straddled one of those hoses to water down the rock.

"Those ten days were filled with challenges that required one creative solution after another. Nine days later, the night before the airport opened, National Car Rental was the only agency that had cars on the lot.

"The key to our success was having the courage to take on any job then being creative in our approach to getting it done."

Carolyn Stradley

Carolyn Stradley, founder of C&S Paving, Inc., recalls the job that challenged her imagination and skill but left her flying high.

Your Personal Action Plan

Tapping Your Creativity

Pursuing a goal is a constantly evolving process. No one who has ever followed a dream has taken a direct, unobstructed path and arrived at his or her destination effortlessly and on time. Following a dream is not a direct highway but a bumpy road full of twists and turns and occasional roadblocks. The journey requires modifications and adjustments in both thought and action, not just once, but over and over. And that means you must be flexible and creative.

Think of yourself as a well-trained pilot. Aviation experts say that a typical flight from New York to Hawaii is slightly off course 90 percent of the time. The pilot or computer must constantly make minor adjustments until the flight finally arrives at its destination. The people in this book became superb pilots of their own destinies; they perpetually modified their courses, adjusted their instruments to suit the changing weather patterns, and responded to every challenge with a flexible, creative attitude that assured their success.

Step 1: Develop Your Inborn Creativity

Creativity Is a Muscle

"Imagination is more important than knowledge." That's what Albert Einstein said, and he should have known. Arguably, Einstein was one of the most intelligent people who ever lived. He solved some of the greatest riddles of science, riddles that had confounded other scientists for centuries. Einstein was a master problem solver, yet he often said that his greatest asset in solving problems was not his intellect but his imagination.

The good news is you don't have to be as imaginative as Einstein to be an effective problem solver. All people have an abundance of creativity within themselves to solve any problem that arises. The challenge is to keep your mind strong and flexible. Your mind functions like a muscle. When you don't use it, it loses its ability to perform. To become an unstoppable problem solver, you must regularly exercise your brain, just as you exercise your body. Exercising your mind might require spending less time in front of the television set and more time thinking, creating, and brainstorming with others on how you can identify a solution to your challenges.

Exercise for Expanding Your Creativity

One of my favorite exercises that illustrates the power of creative problem solving comes from Dr. Robert Schuller. He's used the exercise in seminars for more than thirty years, and thousands of people have benefited from its power. He calls the exercise "Playing the Possibility Thinking Game."

To complete the exercise, you need only a pencil and sheet of paper. First, identify a problem and write the problem across the top of the sheet. Then write the numbers 1 through 10 vertically down the left side of the sheet of paper. Finally, write ten possible solutions to your problem.

The purpose of the exercise is to stretch your imagination and tap unconscious resources. Schuller first used it on himself when he was trying to start a new church in California and was told there was no empty hall he could rent. The possibilities he wrote on his list of ten—all of which emerged intuitively—included renting a school building, a mortuary, or a drive-in theater.

As he jotted down his ideas, Schuller was amazed at the sudden shift in his attitude. At first, thinking of solutions was difficult. But as he completed the exercise, the word "impossible" began to sound ignorant and irresponsible. In that instant, the world seemed full of possibilities again. His dream and his belief in that dream had been completely renewed.

The next step in the exercise is to examine each solution and cross out the ones that don't lead anywhere. In Schuller's case, he crossed out eight solutions before he reached the one that finally worked—a drive-in theater. By spontaneously jotting down ideas that were based on nothing but intuition and imagination, some of which even seemed a little crazy, Schuller found a solution to a major problem.

I used this same exercise with my husband. He is a general contractor, and his business has peaks and valleys. At the time, he was approaching a major valley. He was completing a major contract, and no new contracts were on the horizon. I suggested that he list ten people he could call and ask for referrals. He resisted, arguing that he didn't know ten people who could refer work to him. As we continued to brainstorm, we came up with ten names within about thirty minutes. Out of those ten people, he got leads that developed into two new contracts.

Action: Apply this exercise to one of your current problems. Perhaps you're looking for a way to fund a new business, identify people who can help you launch a product, or determine the solution to a community problem. Write down ten different ways you could approach the problem and reach a solution. Make sure they are viable options, but stretch your imagination.

Remember, the solution to every problem lies within you. You may need a few minutes of quiet time to complete the exercise effectively, or you may need to brainstorm possible solutions with a friend. Feel free to do whatever you think is necessary to connect with your inner knowing. When you've completed the exercise, you should find that the solutions you have found will renew your sense of possibility and commitment to your goal.

STEP 2: BE FLEXIBLE

> ■ **"Your imagination is the preview to life's coming attractions."**
>
> ***—Albert Einstein***

"Creative," "flexible," "imaginative"—these three words are almost interchangeable. If you are creative, you can think of alternative ways to work around problems, ways that align with your own skills and reflect your values. If you are flexible, you are able and willing to change and modify plans; you adjust to new circumstances and needs. If you are imaginative, you envision what is not and what can be—you see in your mind what you haven't yet seen in the material world. All three words refer to your willingness to experiment with new approaches and fresh solutions. When you have these qualities, you will bend and not break when challenges arise.

When a great wind blows, that which is rigid will snap and break. That which is flexible will bend. When the wind dies down and calm returns, the flexible will rise again.

We see almost limitless creativity in inventors. We have all read the stories of people like the Wright brothers, Eli Whitney, Thomas Edison, and Henry Ford. These people triumphed by using imagination and flexibility. They experimented with new materials and techniques that often seemed unrealistic or preposterous at the time. For years, they suffered failure after failure, but they never felt regret. Each time they simply abandoned what did not work, revised their theories, and continued to look for what would work. They were flexible and humble enough to learn from other people's ideas and experiments and to adapt them to their own projects.

Brian Tracy, business writer and consultant, says that to create a successful product, the product need be only 5 percent different from existing products. If the product is too different, it may be "ahead of its time," and consumers may not be ready for it. Ideas are products too. Therefore, it is possible that a creative idea need be only *slightly* different to yield significant results. Anita Roddick's story illustrates the value of a slight change in an idea. She entered the cosmetics field at a time when it had been thriving for years and was dominated by hugely successful corporations. Anita's product was not totally different from theirs, but the natural ingredients and packaging of The Body Shop products gave her the slight difference she needed to succeed.

Unstoppable people always find their way over, around, or under every barrier that confronts them. A brick wall is intimidating, but it is not insurmountable. Unstoppable people believe there's a solution to every problem if they just keep searching.

No one is asking you to become as creative as Shakespeare, as flexible as Houdini, or as imaginative as da Vinci. But you may be surprised at how much exists within you. Dip into your well of creativity. Apply imagination, creativity, and flexibility to the challenges that inevitably appear as you proceed toward your goal. If you tap only 5 percent of your potential, you are on your way to being 100 percent unstoppable.

> ■ **"We are told never to cross a bridge til we come to it, but this world is owned by (people) who have 'crossed bridges' in their imagination far ahead of the crowd."**
>
> —*Speakers Library*

UNSTOPPABLE

An Inventor is a crackpot who suddenly becomes a genius when his idea catches on.

Characteristic Seven

PERSEVERANCE Rewards

If you internalize only one lesson from this entire book, let it be this one: Perseverance Rewards! Every lesson and personality characteristic you've read about in the *Unstoppable* stories offers an important key to success. But the ultimate key—the one that most dramatically separates the achiever from the nonachiever—is perseverance. The people in this book are a living testament to the power of perseverance. If you incorporate only perseverance and none of the other characteristics, your journey toward your goal will certainly be slower and longer, but you will still have a solid chance of arriving there.

Note that the individuals in this last chapter are not superheroes but ordinary human beings with extraordinary tenacity. Observe how they persevered through hardships. What was their attitude? What kept them going?

To assist you in developing unstoppable perseverance, "Your Personal Action Plan" reveals four powerful strategies that will enable you to go the distance until your dream becomes a reality.

■ **"If I were asked to give what I consider the singlemost useful bit of advice for all humanity it would be this: Expect trouble as an inevitable part of life and when it comes, hold your head high, look it squarely in the eye and say, I will be bigger than you. You cannot defeat me."**

—Ann Landers

■ UNSTOPPABLE ■

Door-to-Door Hero

Walking Miles to Stand on His Own Two Feet

He is one of hundreds of thousands in the United States who make their living in sales. Like the rest of them, he rises early each morning to prepare himself for the day ahead. Unlike them, it takes him three hours just to dress and travel to his territory.

No matter how bad the pain, Bill Porter sticks to his grueling routine. Work is everything to Bill: it's his means of survival. But work is also a large part of his worth as a human being, a worth the world once refused to see. Years ago, Bill realized he had a choice: he could be a victim or he could refuse to be one. When he is working, he is not a victim; he is a salesman.

Bill was born in 1932 and the delivery was difficult. The doctors used forceps and accidentally crushed a section of Bill's brain. The result of the injury was that Bill developed cerebral palsy, a disorder of the nervous system that affects Bill's ability to talk, walk, and fully control his limbs. As Bill grew up, people assumed he was mentally deficient. State agencies labeled him "unemployable." Experts said he could never work.

But social service agencies have no way of measuring the human spirit. The agencies saw only what Bill could not do. Thanks to the support of his mother, Bill focused on what he could do. Over and over she told him, "You can do it. You can work and become independent."

Believing the words of his mother, Bill focused on a sales career. He never considered his condition a "disability." He applied first to the Fuller Brush Company, but the company turned him down, saying he couldn't carry a sample case. The Watkins Company said the same. But Bill persisted, vowing he could do the job, and the Watkins Company finally relented on one condition: Bill had to accept the territory of Portland, Oregon, that no one else wanted. It was an opportunity, and Bill took it.

It took Bill four tries before he mustered the courage to ring that first doorbell in 1959. The person who answered was not interested. Neither was the next one, or the next. But Bill's life had forced him to develop strong survival skills. If customers weren't interested, he'd simply come back again and again until he found a product the customers wanted to buy.

For thirty-eight years, his daily routine has been virtually the same. Every morning, on the way to his territory, Bill stops at a shoeshine stand to have his shoelaces tied; his hands are too twisted for him to do it himself. Then he stops at a hotel where the doorman buttons Bill's top shirt button and clips on his tie so Bill can look his best.

Each day, in good weather and bad, Bill covers 10 miles, hauling his heavy sample case up and down hills, his useless right arm tucked behind him. It takes three months, but he knocks on every door in his territory. When he closes a sale, his customers fill out the order form because Bill has difficulty holding a pen.

He returns home from a fourteen-hour day exhausted, his joints aching, and often his head pounding with a migraine. Every few weeks, he types up directions for the woman he hired to make his deliveries. Because he can use only one finger, that simple task usually takes him ten hours. When he finally retires for the night, he sets his alarm clock for 4:45 the next morning.

Over the years, more and more doors stayed open to Bill, and his sales slowly increased. After twenty-four years and millions of knocked-on doors, he finally achieved his goal: He was recognized as the top salesperson in the Watkins Company's western division. He's been a top performer ever since.

Bill is in his sixties now. Although the Watkins Company has 60,000 people who sell the company's household products, Bill is the only one who still sells door-to-door. Most people now buy the items Bill sells in bulk from discount stores, making his job increasingly more difficult. Despite the changing buyer trends, Bill never makes excuses, never complains. He simply continues to do what he does best—getting out in his territory and taking care of his customers.

In the summer of 1996, the Watkins Company held its national convention. This time Bill didn't have to knock on any door or convince anybody to buy his product. This time Bill was the product: the best in the history of the company. Watkins paid tribute to Bill's remarkable courage and outstanding achievement as a human being by making him the first recipient of the prestigious Special Chairman's Award for Dedication and Commitment, an honor that will be bestowed in the future only on rare occasions to an individual who demonstrates qualities similar to those possessed by Bill Porter.

During the presentation, Bill's co-workers rose to their feet with a thunderous standing ovation. The cheers and tears lasted five minutes. Irwin Jacobs, CEO of Watkins, told his employees, "Bill represents the possibilities of what life can be if a person has a goal in mind, then puts his or her heart, soul, and mind into meeting the goal."

That night there was no pain in Bill Porter's eyes. There was only pride.

■ **"Decide what you want out of life; look on the positive side; and never give up until you achieve it."**

—Bill Porter

He just won't take no for an answer!

UNSTOPPABLE

From Rolling Dough to Rolling in Dough

An Entrepreneur Redefines Failure—and Succeeds

Tom Monaghan has had at least a hundred "excuses" for failing in business—from growing up in orphanages and detention homes, to starting a business with no business sense, expanding too soon, going broke, losing everything, building it back up, and almost losing it again.

But what's incredible about Tom Monaghan is that he's never used any excuse. The way he sees it, you haven't failed until you've flat out given up.

His business story begins when he was a college student. In 1960, Tom and his brother Jim borrowed $900 and opened a pizza parlor near the campus of Eastern Michigan University in Ypsilanti, Michigan. As long as classes were in session, the pizza parlor did fine. When school ended, business dropped 75 percent. Through the summer, Tom practically lived at the shop, performing every task himself—making the sauce and fresh dough daily, preparing the vegetable and meat toppings, and dicing cheese for what seemed like hours on end.

Jim, on the other hand, had a secure job at the post office—and less time to devote to the business. When things looked the worst, the partnership began to crumble, and Jim sold his half of the business to Tom in exchange for a 1959 Volkswagen Beetle the brothers had used as a delivery car. "It was a setback," Tom admitted, "but I remained optimistic. I knew that the success of my business was solely mine. And I welcomed it."

Tom would have liked to stay in school, but now, as sole owner, that wasn't an option. With dreams of expansion, he found a man who had run his own pizzeria and had been the first to ever offer free home delivery. Eagerly, Tom offered him a job, but the man would take nothing less than an equal partnership, with a buy-in of $500. Reluctantly, Tom accepted.

Tom and his new partner opened two stores that fall, and by January added a full-service restaurant. The only problem was that Tom still hadn't seen his partner's $500, and everything was still in Tom's name because of his new partner's past bankruptcy. While Tom worked 100 hours a week, drove a rusted-out Rambler, and occasionally cashed his $125 weekly paycheck, his partner went on a spending spree, purchasing cars, property, and making lavish improvements to his house. Despite warnings from Tom's friends that the partner was taking advantage of him, Tom felt his partner's past experience was an asset that he needed. Tom continued to focus on expanding the business. "I believed I wouldn't get hurt if I played it fairly," he said.

A couple of years later, when his partner landed in the hospital and asked to dissolve the partnership, Tom still decided trust was the best business decision. The partnership was so entangled, Tom's lawyer recommended that Tom declare bankruptcy and start over again. Tom adamantly opposed bankruptcy and instead paid his partner $20,000 for his share of the business. Tom knew full well that if his partner ever got into debt again, it would be in his name. Tom wished him well, hoping he'd stay healthy and be able to pay his debt, and went back to work making pizza.

Tom's goal was to be the number one pizzeria and build a reputation for making the best pizza in Ypsilanti. To do so, he instituted strict guidelines regarding the ingredients used in his pizza—all had to be top grade and most importantly, the dough had to be made fresh daily.

His business grew, and slowly Tom paid off some of the bad debt incurred during his former partnership. He worked eighteen-hour days—from 10:00 A.M. until 4:00 A.M. the following morning—seven days a week. After years of dedication, his labor of love allowed him to become current with his bills and actually take a vacation, although it was a working vacation. He and his wife of three years visited every pizzeria they could. Tom's objective was to learn from others how to implement processes that would enable him to handle more business. For Tom, it was an exciting time, and things were really beginning to come together. Tom was eager to grow beyond Ypsilanti and the surrounding area and envisioned expanding Domino's to college towns throughout Michigan.

Two years after his partnership was dissolved, Tom's worst fear became a reality. His ex-partner declared bankruptcy. On Thanksgiving, Tom gave his wife the sobering news. Tom was now responsible for over $75,000 in bad debt. "I had worked so hard to build this business, to make it grow," Tom said, "I couldn't imagine losing it all." He set up a payment plan with the creditors and promised to pay every penny owed. Now more determined than ever to succeed, Tom went back to making pizza.

The next year, while honoring his commitments to his creditors, Tom managed to make $50,000 in net profits. Unfortunately, his profits were short-lived. A devastating fire wiped out his anchor store, and the insurance covered only $13,000 of the $150,000 in damages. Domino's almost went under. But Tom buckled down, cut back wherever he could, and devised ways to cover the fire losses. Once again, Tom went back to making pizza.

On April 1, 1967, the first Domino's franchise opened. Tom's lawyer cautioned him to expand slowly and focus more on managing the business. Tom had no patience for legal details and focused on what he did best, growing the business. Tom continued to drive as hard as ever.

His efforts paid off and a year and a half later, Domino's had risen again. Domino's had grown to a dozen pizzerias, with a dozen more in development. Tom found himself being asked to speak at luncheons about his business success. Domino's was maturing as an organization, and talk of going public was in the air. Tom was having the time of his life. Nearly a decade of working sixteen- to eighteen-hour days, seven days a week, was finally paying off.

His success seemed too good to be true, and it was. Within eighteen months, Tom was out of cash and Domino's was in financial trouble. Checks were bouncing left and right, and his accounting firm quit because Domino's couldn't pay for the service. Without financial statements, Tom had no idea how much he owed; he had trouble believing the $1.5 million figure he saw in the books.

He was on the verge of bankruptcy *again*.

"We had over-expanded and added new stores to territories before the first stores were fully established," Tom explained. "We also made the mistake of sending in untrained managers with no experience to run the new stores and over-staffed our home office."

The business community that had praised him only a few months before now treated him like the town idiot. Desperate to save Domino's, Tom began searching for a merging partner or someone who might see the company's potential. Tom couldn't find one. The bank that carried significant loans for Domino's persuaded Tom to bring in a local businessman who was experienced in turning around struggling companies.

On May 1, 1970, Tom Monaghan lost control of his company. Reluctantly, he assigned his stock partially to the bank and the remaining interest to the local businessman. He entered into an agreement that allowed him to stay on as president—with no authority. Who else could they find willing to work sixteen-hour days, seven days a week, for a $200 weekly paycheck? And seeing that his personal possessions were meager—he still drove an old, beat-up car and the only furniture he owned was a couple of beds and a kitchenette—it was clear he wasn't squandering away money.

Working for someone else was a painful arrangement, but it kept Tom from filing bankruptcy. The new management closed unprofitable pizzerias, cut back on staff, and reorganized what was left. Tom was put in charge of the twelve corporate stores; when he traveled between stores, Tom slept in his car to keep down expenses.

Still, it wasn't enough. After ten months, the local businessman wanted out, deciding Domino's had no future. Since Domino's would probably be in liquidation soon, the businessman agreed to take one of Tom's franchises and give Tom back his stock in return. With Tom back in control of Domino's, he assured his creditors and vendors that he'd pay everyone back if they gave him some time to get back on his feet. Most agreed. His franchisees, however, weren't as sympathetic and filed a class-action antitrust suit against Domino's. When Tom received the legal notice, he sat at his desk and wept.

Over the next nine years, Tom slowly built back his business, paying off every last creditor. For five years, he fought off a bitter, trademark-infringement lawsuit brought by the makers of Domino Sugar. He struggled to survive against a wave of competition within the burgeoning pizza industry.

But Tom did more than just survive. He built an unmatched reputation for Domino's as a restaurant that could deliver a tasty piping-hot pizza, within thirty minutes to the customer's door. This claim made Domino's the largest home delivery pizza business in the world, and Tom became one of the wealthiest entrepreneurs in the country, with 97 percent of the company's stock.

Tom reached that pinnacle of success despite a difficult childhood, the skimpiest of financial resources, and little more than a high school education. Tom had every reason to make excuses, to fail, to quit. But "quit" isn't in Tom Monaghan's vocabulary. "Persistence" is.

■ **"I feel all these setbacks were tools for me to learn from. I used them as stepping-stones and didn't see them as failures. A failure is when you stop trying, and I never did that."**

—Tom Monaghan

UNSTOPPABLE
I'M MAKING A LIST OF ALL THE THINGS I'VE LEARNED IN LIFE...
WELL, ACTUALLY, I'M MAKING TWO LISTS
WHY IS ONE LIST LONGER THAN THE OTHER?
THESE ARE THINGS I'VE LEARNED THE HARD WAY!

■ UNSTOPPABLE ■

If At First You Don't Succeed...

Try, Try (47 Times) Again

Twenty people in the past hour have listened to your sales pitch and hung up the phone. Five banks in a row have rejected your application for a small business loan. Your screenplay has just been returned with another letter that starts, "Thank you for thinking of us but..."

This is the moment you lift up your chin, square your shoulders, and say to yourself, "Maxcy Filer."

Why? Because the first time Maxcy Filer took the California bar exam in 1966 he was thirty-six years old. He didn't pass, so he tried again. And again. And again. And again. He took the bar exam in Los Angeles, San Diego, Riverside, San Francisco, and anywhere else it was given in California. He took the bar when his children were still living at home, and he took it with two of his sons when they had earned their own law school degrees. He took the bar after he started working for his sons as a law clerk in their offices. And he kept taking the bar when he reached an age when most people start thinking about retirement.

And he passed. After twenty-five years, $50,000 in fees for exams and countless review courses, and a total of 144 days spent in testing rooms, he took the bar exam for the forty-eighth time, and he passed. Maxcy was sixty-one.

Why?

"Because I couldn't possibly quit," he explained. "I don't quit. I looked at it from the standpoint that the bar was passable, and one day I would succeed and I wasn't going to give up."

Despite every attempt, Maxcy simply refused to see himself as a failure. He had decided to become an attorney in the 1950s when he realized that law and justice did not always balance for the black man. He watched as Thurgood Marshall, Nathaniel Jones, Lauren Miller, and other attorneys began making changes and decided he wanted to use the law to change society too.

However, it had not been possible for him to go to law school after college. He and his wife, Blondell, had seven children to raise. So it was eight years later when he applied to, and eventually graduated from, Van Norman University.

Maxcy has always felt that he knew the law as well on his third attempt at passing the bar as he did on his forty-eighth attempt. Over the years, he consistently scored in the top 10 percent of the law review courses he took. Maxcy served as a city councilman in Compton where he lived and impressed his sons with his knowledge of law cases in the office, drawing up all the complaints and doing much of the work.

So what was the problem?

Apparently, Maxcy didn't test well. The California bar exam, which has one of the nation's highest failure rates, is partly a writing test, and as Maxcy's sons pointed out, his "syntax" wasn't in the expected "lawyer" style. Maxcy certainly knew his cases, but he also had a tendency to focus on practical rather than academic law issues.

What kept him going long after most people would have switched to another field?

The unwavering support of family and friends, he said. Every time he failed, his wife would immediately type up another application, saying, "You know, Maxcy, you came very close this time. Try it again. I'm sure you'll do it next time."

It helped Maxcy Filer to recall some of his classmates who had been slackers in his school days. Some of those slackers were now practicing law. "So why should I give up?" Maxcy asked himself.

"I had an attitude that every time I took the exam, I was taking it for the first time and that helped," he explained. He also benefited from an unshakable belief that he would eventually pass. "The way I see it, I passed the bar every time I took it. They just didn't pass me."

It was one of Maxcy's sons who opened the envelope that arrived after that forty-eighth attempt. Maxcy had tossed the envelope up on the mantle, just as he had all the others for twenty-five years, and it had remained there, unopened among the family's best china, for hours. Maxcy's son finally opened the envelope, let out a shout, then jumped on his father and began kissing and hugging him. It took Maxcy forty minutes to believe what he was reading: "Congratulations, Mr. Filer…"

During Maxcy's swearing-in ceremony, a thousand of his colleagues were on hand to show their respect for a man whose optimistic spirit and tenacious persistence was like none other they had ever witnessed.

Today Maxcy Filer practices law a half-mile from the courthouse in Compton, California. When he tells clients he'll fight their case to the bitter end, they can be sure he will.

■ **"Keep going. Say 'I will do it' and you will."**

—Maxcy Filer

▪ Something to Think About ▪

Writer David Saperstein's manuscript novel, "Cocoon," was rejected 52 times by agents, publishers, studios, and producers. People told him over and over that "This is a wrinkle story..." "Old people don't buy movie tickets..." "No one cares about old fogies..." This was the first fiction David ever wrote.

After the manuscript was finally optioned for film rights, Richard Zanuck, the film's producer, wouldn't hire him to write the screenplay stating that David was "nobody" and they needed "somebody" to write the script. Five years, and several screenwriters later, the last writer came back to David's original story and the movie got made.

David's insight based on this experience: "Perserverence and belief in yourself is the ONLY name of the game (plus some talent, some luck and lots of patience)."

David's story proves that anyone who keeps on going after 51 rejections, creates their own luck.

You don't have to be the fastest.

UNSTOPPABLE

A Dream Goes to "Waste"

Who Says You Can't Fight City Hall?

When other twelve-year-old girls were on the telephone, giggling about their latest crushes, Laura-Beth Moore was on the line to the mayor trying to change the way things were done in her city. While other girls were strolling the mall, Laura-Beth was canvassing the neighborhood with petitions. During summer vacation, when her classmates were at the movies or with friends, Laura-Beth was at home putting in full days on the phone again, trying to drum up support for a dream she had been told wasn't practical.

What inspired Laura to spend three months of vacation time feverishly working instead of playing? What was it that instilled in her such passion and conviction?

Garbage. Garbage, that is, that had not been recycled.

After seeing the 1990 demonstrations on Earth Day, Laura-Beth became aware that the entire city of Houston, her hometown, had not one recycling program. She resolved to change that. *Without recycling, we are basically throwing away the Earth,* she thought.

With her first inquiries, Laura-Beth seemed to run straight into a wall. The city wouldn't return her calls. City employees told her to have an adult call instead. When she finally reached someone who at least would talk to her, the person didn't seem to care. She tried writing letters instead, asking the mayor if the city could provide curbside recycling. The answer was no, but six months later, she heard Houston was running a test on neighborhood recycling. Hoping it would include her neighborhood, Laura-Beth prepared a petition with hundreds of signatures and delivered it to city hall. Again, the response was no. Citywide recycling was not "cost effective," said the mayor.

"The mayor just blew me off," Laura-Beth recalled. "She basically said, 'You're just a kid.'"

That may have been true, but Laura-Beth had been raised to believe she could do anything if she just kept working at it. "Nothing comes easy," Laura-Beth commented. "You have to work hard for everything. And no matter how small your voice is, I believe you can make a difference."

Sometimes making a difference just involves changing your tactics. Laura-Beth decided that if governmental agencies wouldn't help, perhaps private businesses would. She began calling large recycling companies, hoping they would offer help or advice. But they, too, refused to take the twelve-year-old seriously.

Laura-Beth's mother watched from the sidelines, convinced her daughter would learn a lesson in "biting off more than she could chew" and abandon her crusade. Instead, it was her mother who would learn a lesson about just how determined a twelve-year-old could be.

Laura-Beth persevered without results. With every rejection, she told herself, *That's just one more step that I've taken, one more phone call, one less person to deal with. I'll just move on to the next person until I reach someone who will help.*

Little did she realize that person would have to be herself. Laura-Beth decided to create a recycling plan for her own neighborhood. She spent the summer seeking information and support from companies and agencies, trying to find a way to make the plan pay for itself. When she felt she finally had a solid, workable plan, she took her cause to the neighborhood homeowners' group. The group approved the plan and offered its support.

But one more hurdle remained. Laura-Beth needed a place for neighbors to leave their recyclables, and the local school seemed like the most practical place. Just as before, the principal refused to take her calls. Just as before, Laura-Beth persisted in the face of resistance. For months, she made countless phone calls until a group of parents finally rallied to her aid and convinced the principal to cooperate.

"Even if I hadn't gotten help, there's no doubt in my mind I'd still be plugging away. I was going to make this happen no matter how much time it took," explained Laura-Beth.

On the first collection day in the spring of 1991, hundreds of residents dropped off their recyclable trash. Several volunteers showed up with their pick-up trucks to collect the trash and drive it to the recycling plant. For about three months, the recycling program appeared to be successful. Then the number of volunteers started dwindling. Laura-Beth came up with another idea. Using her own allowance of $20 a month, she rented a truck and recruited a volunteer to drive the paper, tin, aluminum, glass, and plastic across town to the recycling companies.

Two years later, the truck still makes at least one trip a month, and the program is more than self-supporting. On one Saturday alone the truck carried off 17 tons of material that would have been in a landfill but is now on its way to be recycled into usable products.

A few years after the recycling program was up and running, Houston's new mayor decided she'd like similar programs in other neighborhoods. When the mayor asked city officials to write the plan, they knew exactly where to turn. This time it was the city making the phone call, and the city was calling Laura-Beth Moore.

■ **"Don't ever give up; take it all the way. Somebody will finally see it your way, and they will help you."**

—Laura-Beth Moore

I'm very good at visualizing my success...
but other people are equally as good
at visualizing my failure.

▪ In Their Own Words ▪

"As far back as I can remember, *I wanted a career in show business. And as far back as I can remember, people were telling me no.*

"On December 7, 1958, I walked into The Showbar in Boston. I was to be paid $125 for the week—two shows a night. I had already checked into the hotel across the street. It was a dirty, horrible place, but I didn't care. This was my first job.

"I had already been turned down by every agent in New York when I found Harry Brent. He was the man willing to work with me, mold my act, and ultimately book me into The Showbar as 'Pepper January...Comedy With Spice!' Things were really looking up—or so I thought. After the first show, the manager called me over. 'Hey, Pepper,' he said, 'you're fired.'

"I was devastated. Fired! Fired from my first job! I went back to my crummy hotel room and collapsed. I literally could not stop crying. I cried as I stood under the shower in that filthy tub, my feet protected with socks, the curtain open so that the killer from Psycho could not stab me! Standing in that dirt-blackened tub, I no longer knew whether the thing inside me struggling to get out was talent or only an obsession. But I didn't give in.

"Soon I was booked and fired from my second job. Harry Brent also left me, taking the name 'Pepper January' with him. 'Women comics I can find,' he explained, 'but a name like that is hard to come by!' Meanwhile, I was back to square one.

"I tried everything and called on everyone. Very little worked and everyone said no. My own mother said, 'You have no talent. You're throwing your life away.' One of the most powerful theatrical agents in the business told me, 'You're too old. If you were going to make it, you would have made it by now.' The talent coordinator for the Tonight Show said, 'We just don't think you'd work on TV.' The verdict certainly seemed to be in, but I just couldn't quit.

"I had no money. My office was a phone booth in Grand Central Station. I lived out of one small suitcase and slept in my car while my father threatened to have me committed to Bellevue. All in all—not an easy time. It did, however, serve to shape the determination and an inner strength I have called on in my life many times since.

"Children especially, I believe, sometimes see success as a 'lucky lottery ticket' that one chances upon. And that is why I think it is important to note that in my case, I was thirty-one years old. Thirty-one years of hearing 'no.' Thirty-one long years before the acceptance began. And that even in my darkest moments, I knew instinctively that my unyielding drive was my most important asset. Perseverance will always be just as important—important as talent.

"Never stop believing! Never give up! Never quit! Never."

Joan Rivers is a comedienne, author, actress, playwright, businesswoman, and mother, but is perhaps best-known to audiences for her Emmy Award-winning TV talk show. The first sole permanent guest hostess of The Tonight Show, Rivers currently hosts E! Entertainment Television's "Fashion Reviews" and, along with her daughter, Melissa, hosts E!'s "live," pre-show commentary for the Academy Awards, Golden Globe Awards, and Emmy Awards telecasts.

Excerpted with permission from *Storms of Perfection*, by Andy Andrews

▪ In Their Own Words ▪

"What business does a former housewife *from Schenectady have behind the wheel of a race car? None, if you asked just about everyone that was in my life at the time. But I saw it differently.*

"All I ever wanted to do was race cars, but in the mid-60s, that was no way for a woman to make a living. The sport of drag racing was completely male-dominated at the time, and everyone told me it was impossible for a woman to compete. Auto manufacturers refused to sponsor me, The National Hot Rod Association (NHRA) didn't take me seriously and hoped I would go away. But it didn't happen. I'm a fighter.

"I persevered, and little by little, I moved closer to my dream. Because we had no sponsors, my first husband and I came up with a plan for building our own car with him serving as the maintenance crew. To enter the racing circuit we needed permission from the NHRA, which governs all national racing events. Even after meeting every qualification they had, we had to fight hard to get the NHRA to reverse its long-standing policy against women racing in the dragster class.

"We had so many obstacles to overcome and yet, we hadn't even competed in one national race. In 1970, I finally got my opportunity and competed at the US Nationals in Indianapolis where we missed qualifying by two one-hundreths of a second. This showed that we were serious competitors. I continued to tour and in 1976 became the first woman drag racer to win a NHRA national event. The following year, I became the first-ever drag racer to win three national events back to back in my class.

"I persevered against the odds and against the rules because I believed in my dreams. It would have been more difficult for me to live with that unfulfilled passion than it was to fight to make it happen.

"Because I held true to my dreams, today I know the feeling of a 5,000 horsepower engine, the feeling of driving over 300 miles-per-hour, and most importantly I know the feeling of being a champion."

Shirley Muldowney

Shirley Muldowney now competes on the IHRA circuit, International Hot Rod Association, and fills the remainder of her schedule with invitational races. Shirley holds numerous distinguishing records including winning the World Championship four times. She also set and reset the IHRA speed record four times in 1997 and currently holds the record at 303.70 mph. The United States Sports Academy voted Shirley Muldowney as one of the top 25 professional female athletes in the last 25 years.

Your Personal Action Plan

Perseverance Rewards Your Efforts

"N*ever...Never...Never quit*"

Winston Churchill offered those four words of advice after years of military blunders and political failures that would have doomed the career of the average statesman. Instead, Churchill went on to become the prime minister of England and a major Allied leader during World War II.

The need for persistence is as true for the business entrepreneur as it is for the politician; persistence is as critical to the success of an artist as it is to a minister.

The people you have read about in this book were not superheroes; they were not blessed with special gifts and strengths that the rest of us lack. They are ordinary human beings with extraordinary tenacity. They persevered through hardships with physical, mental, and emotional suffering because they had already internalized many of the key lessons from this book: the power of purpose, passion, faith, preparedness, creativity, building a support team, and perseverance. Consciously or unconsciously, these people used these powerful strategies, which enabled them to go the distance until their dreams became realities.

STEP 1. FOCUS ON YOUR GOAL

Unstoppable achievers keep their eyes on the target at all times. They often use visual keys to remind them through the day of the goal they're working toward.

Olympic decathlon gold medalist Bruce Jenner even arranged his entire apartment so it would remind him every day of his goal. He put equipment from each of the ten sports in the decathlon in places where he couldn't help but encounter them during his non training hours. Since the high hurdle was his weakest skill, he placed a hurdle right in the middle of the living room, where he had to step over it as many as thirty times a day. His doorstop was an iron shot. His barbells were on the patio. Vaulting poles and javelins rose from behind the couch. And his closets held the uniforms of his sport: sweat suits and running shoes. The unusual decor, Bruce said, helped him improve his form as he prepared for (and won!) the Olympic gold medal.

Action: Create a constant reminder of your goal. By now, I'm hoping you've identified your purpose, written your statement of calling, and created a dream that evokes your passion. The next step is to keep that dream and the goals that support it at the forefront of your mind. Here are just a few of the many ways you could do so:

- Write your statement of calling and goals on note cards or Post-It Notes and strategically place them throughout your house and office.
- Record your statement of calling and goals on an audio cassette and play the tape as you're driving, doing chores, resting, or meditating.

- Put your goals on the screen saver of your computer.

For example, I entered my top goals on my computer and printed them on decorative papers. I then hung the papers in my office, on my bedroom mirror, and even on my refrigerator. I laminated one copy, hole-punched it, and placed it in the front of my day-planner. My goals are virtually always in sight and help me to stay focused on what's most important to me.

You can surround yourself with your dream and build your commitment in hundreds of ways. The method you choose is not important. What is important is to do something! Bruce Jenner's methods were exceptionally imaginative and even extreme—but so were the results. If you make the effort to remain as constantly focused as he was, nothing can stop you.

Sir Isaac Newton was asked how he discovered the law of gravity and he replied, "*By thinking about it all the time*."

STEP 2: ACCEPT FAILURES AS LEARNING EXPERIENCES

> **"Our greatest glory is not in never failing, but in rising every time we fail."**
>
> *—Confucius*

Unstoppable people don't believe in failure. They see mistakes as opportunities to learn and develop new skills and strategies, not as failure. Failure implies waste, that nothing has been gained. On the contrary, people can gain much from every mistake and setback along the road to success. Mistakes and failures are inevitable and even essential; they are evidence of action—that you are doing something. The more mistakes you make, the greater your chance of succeeding. Failures indicate a willingness to experiment and take risks. Unstoppable people know that each failure brings them a step closer to achieving their dreams.

■ **"Many people dream of success. To me, success can be achieved only through repeated failure and introspection. In fact, success represents the 1 percent of your work that results from 99 percent that is called failure."**

—Soichiro Honda

Honda has said what hundreds of other achievers have said before him. You may remember that Edison said he would never have invented the light bulb without first failing at 4,000 experiments. Biologist Thomas Huxley said failure was of the "greatest practical benefit" to him. Susan B. Anthony said simply that failure is "impossible." Anton Chekhov said one would have to be a god to tell the difference between failure and success.

History is full of stories that support Chekhov's view. When Christopher Columbus made a mistake in his calculations and stumbled across the New World when he hoped to find Asia, was he a failure or a success?

An old adage says "the arrow that hits the bull's eye is the result of a hundred misses." I'm sure everyone in this book would agree. It's through adversity and failure that we ultimately win. Being able to see failure as an opportunity for learning and improvement is critical to becoming unstoppable. People who can't bear a moment of failure have doomed themselves to mediocrity, for they'll never be able to push themselves past a point that is uncomfortable or unfamiliar. Yet it is beyond that point where success dwells.

Jim Rohn, author and professional speaker, said "If you're not willing to risk the unusual, you will have to settle for the ordinary."

Don't settle.

> ■ **"Far better is it to dare mighty things, to win glorious triumphs even though checkered by failure, than to rank with those poor spirits who neither enjoy nor suffer much because they live in the gray twilight that knows neither victory nor defeat."**
>
> *—Theodore Roosevelt*

UNSTOPPABLE "FAILURES"

- **Brooks Robinson,** called the greatest third baseman of all times, was sent back to the minors after a disappointing year in the majors.
- **Howard Head,** the inventor who revolutionized the sports of skiing and tennis, spent eighteen months building six pairs of metal skis, only to watch a skeptical ski pro break them in thirty minutes. It took four years and forty more handmade pairs of skis until he finally made a pair that couldn't be broken.
- After releasing her first album in 1978, **Amy Grant** went on her first promotional tour. One of her appearances at a book signing and record store included signing autographs and singing for ninety minutes. The manager had sent out 1,200 engraved invitations to promote Amy's performance and he was expecting a large turnout. Not one person showed up. Not even store customers. For ninety minutes, Amy sang to a one-person audience, the store manager.
- After only one season on the air, ***Baywatch*** joined the hundreds of other television shows that are canceled their first year

on the air. But *Baywatch* had something the other hundreds of shows didn't: David Hasselhoff. He and a few friends believed they had a marketable show and purchased the rights themselves. They sold *Baywatch* to an U.S. distributor and a European syndicator; the series now airs in over 140 countries.

- **Ted Koppel** once said he could have wallpapered his walls with the rejections he received in his pursuit of a job as foreign correspondent. At one point, he was so desperate for a job that he interviewed with advertising firms because he knew he could at least write. Even the advertising firms wouldn't hire him.
- **Randy Travis** was turned down more than once by every recording company in Nashville.
- After one of **Katie Couric's** early television news appearances, the president of CNN told her he never wanted to see her on camera again.

Step 3. Be Patient—Cultivate a Long-term Mentality

We live in a society that demands and has grown accustomed to instant gratification. Most people today lack the patience necessary to achieve their goals. Unfortunately, there are no fast-food outlets serving up our dreams. Achieving your dream takes time. Every moment you are working, you can take comfort in realizing you are moving closer and closer to your dream. That work, the journey itself, is the adventure and half of the reward. Don't shortchange it.

■ **"Don't let me ever hear you use the word 'impossible.' If I've learned anything over the course of my career, there's no such thing as impossible. Overnight, the impossible may not be possible. But over time, the impossible certainly becomes possible."**

—Earl Graves

Step 4: Never Quit

Ann Landers advises us to "expect trouble as an inevitable part of life. When it comes, hold your head high, look it squarely in the eye and say, 'I will be bigger than you. You cannot defeat me.'"

The consistent message from each of the individuals in this book is to pursue your dream with confidence and never, never, never quit. If you don't give up, you simply cannot fail. Not only will you achieve your dreams, but the combination of your commitment, courage, and faith will rise as the greatest triumph of all.

■ **"It took me fifteen years to discover that I had no talent for writing, but I couldn't give it up because by then I was too famous."**

—Robert Benchley

conclusion

YOUR LEGACY: A Bold Unstoppable Spirit!

Even though you and I may have never met, I believe that we are kindred spirits. Your longing to grow and to create a rich and meaningful life has brought us together. No matter where you are in your life, you desire more. Regardless of the success you may be currently experiencing, you believe deep in your soul that you are destined for far greater things.

It is important to realize that you possess everything you need to achieve your own unique form of greatness—whether you desire to be an outstanding professional, entrepreneur, citizen, or parent. Like the people in this book, you too can become unstoppable. By taking responsibility for your life and your future and refusing to allow any circumstance, no matter how formidable, to be an excuse for failure, you can create your own unstoppable legacy.

All things, even the seemingly impossible, can be accomplished if you:

- Devote yourself to your true purpose
- Follow your heart's passion
- Believe in yourself and your ideas
- Prepare for challenges
- Ask for help and the support of others
- Creatively seek solutions
- Persevere, no matter what the challenges

Now that you have identified real-life mentors that not only inspire you but show you how to become unstoppable, and you've completed "Your Personal Action Plan" designed to help you develop the characteristics necessary to achieve your goal, it's time for action. There will never be a better time for you to begin than this very moment. Do it now! Don't procrastinate. Remember the law of inertia: a body at rest tends to stay at rest; a body in motion tends to stay in motion. A basic law of physics is on your side. Even the smallest action can multiply into a driving force.

You have met individuals who have accomplished the remarkable. One teenage boy walked thousands of miles across Africa. All of the people in this book walked beyond their pain and failures. One woman rose above the prejudice against her physical being. All of them rose above the slavery of security and approval. One woman challenged the giants of the beauty industry. All of them conquered the tyrants of skepticism and doubt. Two of these women broke through the gender barriers and entered fields previously dominated by men. All of them broke through the barriers of their own fears and excuses. One man solved an "unsolvable" problem. All of them built bridges from the world of the impossible to the world of the possible.

All of them were unstoppable. And you can be one of them.

It is my hope that this book has rekindled a lost dream, revitalized an existing one, and inspired you to pursue your goals with greater energy and deeper resolve. Draw strength from our unstoppable examples. Follow the path the people in this book have charted before you. See your vision become a reality. Be bold. Be unstoppable!

.unstoppable.

"They appear as giants, driven to achieve.
Not of the ordinary fabric weaved.
When faced with adversity and obstacles too,
They refuse to be stopped, continue to barrel through.

What keeps them going, what holds them on track,
When so many others are wont to turn back?
How are they different? What sets them apart?
Could I barrel through, too, with such strength in my heart?

The truth is so simple, it's hard to admit it.
They're not lucky or blessed or specially gifted.
Like anyone else, they too have doubts and fears,
But the difference with them, is how they live their years.

They live with Purpose, a quest that gives rise
To pursuing what counts with no compromise.
Burning with passion, turning work into love,
Enlisting support from around and above.

The whole is envisioned with the end in mind,
Carefully planned, continuously refined.
When challenges loom, and seem to prevail
They chart a new course, alter their sail.

They cling to their faith, the vision persists
They simply will not cease or desist.
Call them stubborn, they refuse to give in
They persist, persevere—and yes, they do win.

If you will pursue the dream of your heart
And follow their path, don't wait to start
You'll realize your dreams, break through all obstacles!
And become as they are, triumphant—Unstoppable!"

—Cynthia Kersey
UNSTOPPABLE

Appendix

Tips for Starting Your Own Mastermind Group

Sherry Phelan has developed six steps for developing a powerful mastermind group that can help you achieve your goals.

Step 1. Carefully Select Team Members

The optimal number of members in a mastermind group is six to eight. Look for individuals who can commit to the group for at least a year who will make their best efforts to attend every meeting. Trust and rapport take time to develop. Results are created over time.

Determine the mix of skills and levels of experience you'd like to include in the group. Target individuals who meet your requirements and will commit themselves. Ideal members are noncompetitors, open and honest about their strengths and needs, willing to contribute their expertise freely, and able to keep confidences. New members must be unanimously approved by the group.

Step 2. Set a Regular Meeting Time

If possible, meetings should be held on the same day, twice each month. For example, the meetings could be held on the first and third Saturdays of each month. This frequency of meetings encourages steady progress. The two weeks between meetings allows members time to implement ideas, give birth to new ideas discussed during the previous meeting, develop new ideas to introduce to the group, and identify issues and questions to raise at the next meeting.

Ideally, meetings should last between two and two and a half hours. Some people prefer morning meetings. People are usually more alert, and you will have enough time to involve every member. To get the most out of the limited time, however, it is important that each member speak succinctly and listen receptively.

Step 3. Make a Pact

In the first meeting, establish the rules of the team. Address items such as confidentiality, starting on time, and regular attendance. You might also want to discuss issues of communication and participation. Write up an agreement for existing and new members to sign.

Step 4. Develop Quarterly Action Plans

In one meeting each quarter, team members should set goals and develop action plans. These quarterly meetings will focus on the team's progress and related issues discussed during the other weekly meetings and on action to be taken between quarterly meetings. Choose one or two priority projects you want to work on each quarter and commit yourself to taking the steps necessary to completing them.

Step 5. Determine Your Meeting Agenda

Your regular meeting agenda should include a celebration of achievements, problem-solving, and accountability for each member. Members must come prepared with issues or questions for the group, as well as with suggestions and solutions for other team members.

During every meeting, each member takes a turn on "the hot seat." Each member is given the same amount of time. Once on the hot seat, the member:

A. Briefly reports an outstanding victory for the week.
B. Reviews the progress and obstacles since the last meeting.
C. Raises a succinct question for the group, providing a very quick background of the problem.
D. Receives and writes down ideas from team members as they brainstorm solutions. The focus at this point is to absorb as much of the group's wisdom as possible. Solutions can be reviewed and evaluated after the meeting.
E. Commits to achieving results by the next meeting.

Step 6: Establish Key Roles for Team Members

Every member plays an important role in creating an effective team. The most critical role is that of the facilitator, which should be the same person at every meeting. The facilitator keeps the process organized, focused, and moving toward solutions. Using an outside facilitator can encourage full participation. Another role is that of the timer, who announces when the "hot seat" time is up for each person.

Sherry Phelan is available for keynote presentations, planning and meeting facilitation, and consulting on developing mastermind alliances. She can be reached at TAP Turn-Around Programs, 1869 Midlothian Drive, Altadena, CA 91001. Telephone: 626-296-6696.

Opportunity to Give

Help Create an Unstoppable Success Story for Someone Else

For every success story you read about in Unstoppable, there are thousands of other stories just waiting to be written. Often a family or a child just needs a helping hand to improve their situation, circumstances, and outlook.

One organization that is providing this helping hand is Habitat for Humanity International. Over the past twenty years, Habitat for Humanity has—with the financial help of generous donors and the labor of people from all walks of life—built over 60,000 homes for families living in sub-standard or dangerous conditions. This powerful demonstration of love in action has provided a step up for countless men, women, and children.

- A Vietnam veteran who was jobless, homeless, and illiterate transformed his life and his family's future just three years after moving into his Habitat-built home. His children, who were failing in school, began getting straight A's with certificates for academic achievement. One daughter now says she wants to go to medical school, all because of the change a Habitat home made in their lives.
- The very first house Habitat ever built was for a family whose father was so illiterate he couldn't even sign the mortgage. But all five of

the children raised in that Habitat home are successful today and active in professions such as nursing, law, and counseling.

- A Habitat home owner who discovered Habitat for Humanity from a newspaper she was stuffing into a broken window of her dilapidated trailer home, created a new life for her family and her husband. Her children began to take an interest in improving their own lives through school, her husband's heart condition—aggravated by poor living conditions and hours of back-breaking, low-income work—began to rapidly improve, and the woman now earns her own income, all because of a Habitat home.

With more than two million poor families in the United States who must, with their children, survive in severely sub-standard housing (or none at all), Habitat for Humanity's goal is to make decent shelter a matter of conscience for every family who goes to sleep at night in a safe, comfortable, and clean environment. Habitat's no-profit, no-interest, self-help formula provides the means for those without hope to own a decent home and create a solid foundation upon which to build a life, a family, and a stable future.

Author Cynthia Kersey has chosen Habitat for Humanity International as her charity of choice for *Unstoppable* and is actively supporting it by offering her time, expertise, and energy to help fulfill its mission. As well, Ms. Kersey will donate a percentage of her royalties from *Unstoppable* to help further this important work.

We hope you will join us and explore the opportunities to support Habitat for Humanity through donations of time and/or money. Call or write now and find out how you can give the gift of hope to a family in need of a decent place to live.

Habitat for Humanity International
121 Habitat Street
Americus, GA 31709-3423
1-800-422-4828

To Be Continued

We're already working on the sequel to *Unstoppable*. We plan to publish a new *Unstoppable* book every year including special editions for women, children, salespeople, entrepreneurs, people from everyday life, etc. Whenever I talk to people about *Unstoppable*, many times their first response is, "I should be in your next book—Let me tell you my story" or "I know someone who is absolutely unstoppable."

If you feel the same way, send me your story. Or you may have discovered other unstoppable people through stories you've read in your local newspaper, magazine, or the company in which you work.

I'd love to hear from you. Please send me your personal unstoppable story or the story of someone that you've heard about. Be sure to include the name and contact information of the unstoppable individual. If you read about this person or saw their story on television, reference the source and date it was printed or aired. Please be sure to include your name, return address, business or home phone, fax, and email address.

Cynthia Kersey
P.O. Box 877
Agoura Hills, CA 91376-0877
Fax: 818-880-9237
cynthia@unstoppable.net
website: www.unstoppable.net

JOIN OUR UNSTOPPABLE NETWORK...

Pursuing your dreams may feel lonely at times, but it doesn't have to. There are tens of thousands of individuals who, just like you, are committed to becoming unstoppable in achieving their dreams and goals.

To support you on your unstoppable journey, I'd like to invite you to **join our community of unstoppable people.** When you join, you'll receive a free membership kit filled with information and tools to help you with your daily commitment to achieving your unique purpose and goals in life.

Additionally, you will receive exclusive notification for special networking opportunities in your area, announcements on upcoming conferences where you can meet other unstoppable individuals, and continuing information on unstoppable publications, products and services that will assist you in your pursuits.

Remember, the stronger your team, the more unstoppable you become. Join me and become a member of this unique network of individuals.

YOUR MEMBERSHIP AND NEW MEMBER KIT ARE FREE!

To receive your FREE membership and new member kit, please send a self-addressed stamped envelope (with two-ounce postage) to: **Cynthia Kersey, P.O. Box 877, Agoura Hills, CA 91376-0877.** Please include your phone number, fax and e-mail address.

Don't miss this opportunity to draw on a vast number of people and resources that can help you with your unstoppable endeavors.

Create Your Own Unstoppable Success Story with Cynthia Kersey's Audio Program

"Your Unstoppable Journey"

30 Days to Creating the Unstoppable You!

If you have yet to get clear on your unique calling...If you are concerned about looking back on a life that lacks meaning...If you believe you are destined for far greater things than you are experiencing in life, *YOUR UNSTOPPABLE JOURNEY—a 30-day audio program*—is for you! Not only will it help you discover specifically what you were put on this planet to do, you'll create an action plan to make it happen.

As part of this powerful program, you'll receive:

***Your Unstoppable Journey* Audio Program... A 30-day program** delivered in "bite-size" sessions on eight audio cassettes, details the seven characteristics of Unstoppable people and shows you how to make them come alive in your life—in 15 minutes or less each day!

***Your Unstoppable Journey* Personal Action Guide... An 80-page workbook** including 30 daily written action items that will walk you, step-by-step, through developing unstoppable characteristics in your own life.

***Passport to Your Unstoppable Journey...* A 32-page passport-sized booklet** containing time-tested wisdom certain to motivate you, inspire you and keep you on your unstoppable course!

Call today to receive this extraordinary program at a special price offered to *Unstoppable* readers!

Call TOLL FREE: 888-867-8677
FAX: 818-880-9237
Email: cynthia@unstoppable.net

About the Author

No one would have been more surprised that I, if you had told me a few years ago that I would one day write a book. I had no aspirations whatsoever of becoming a writer. However, I made a discovery three years ago that changed my life forever and out of that discovery this book was borne.

My start in business was less than promising. My career began as a young woman in Cincinnati who could not keep an entry-level job as a secretary and over a period of years, I rose to the top of my field earning a six-figure income at Sprint. Yet, I was still not satisfied with my life. Although I was a "successful" business-woman, selling telecommunications products did not provide me with deep personal satisfaction.

Like many of you may have experienced, I grew increasingly concerned that at the end of my years, I would look back on a life filled with activities, but those activities lacked real meaning and purpose. With each passing day, I became more and more compelled to find my unique calling and engage in a meaningful life's work. Through a process of self-reflection and discovery, I identified the one thing that provided me with the greatest joy—encouraging others. Specifically, encouraging people to believe in themselves more deeply and to pursue their dreams with boldness and passion.

As I thought about what to do for my first project, I considered the areas that had given me the greatest encouragement. I love books and have derived enormous inspiration from reading about individuals who were unstoppable. People who had a dream and despite rejection after rejection and failure after failure finally achieved their goal. Their stories gave me tremendous hope about what was possible for my own life. After reflecting on the impact their lives had on me personally and the courage they gave me to pursue my dream, I became compelled to share their stories with others.

So, I decided to write a book! Now mind you, I had never written anything longer than a college term paper in my entire life, possessed absolutely no contacts in the publishing industry, and had no clue as to what a literary agent even looked like. When I enthusiastically shared my plans with friends and colleagues, many thought I had lost my mind. Some "supportively" reminded me of how difficult it was to jump into another industry when you have no experience and encouraged me to stay in the field I knew best, telecommunications.

While it was clear that I didn't have a great literary background or any experience in writing a book, I did possess an overwhelming passion for my new project. Convinced that this enthusiasm would fuel my efforts to do whatever was necessary to accomplish my goal, I quit my "day" job, cashed in my husband's and my entire life savings and wholeheartedly spent 16 months researching and interviewing hundreds of unstoppable individuals.

Now, I'm not going to say it was easy, but through this process I experienced a passion and a joy that I had never known before in any line of "work." And now, two years later, I am fortunate and grateful to be living my life's calling by sharing this Unstoppable message with you.

It's my sincere desire that this book and the individuals you'll meet will significantly impact your life as they have mine. Allow their stories to open new possibilities in your life and instill in you the overwhelming conviction that you can overcome and achieve anything.

May God bless you as you travel on your own unstoppable journey.

Cynthia

About the Unstoppable Individuals Profiled

I am certain that you were moved by the people you met in this book. Perhaps you'd like to share with them the impact their story has had on your life or are interested in supporting the cause they represent. You can reach them at the addresses below.

Robyn Allan. CYF Consulting Ltd., Denman Place Postal Outlet, P.O. Box 47057, Vancouver B.C. V6G 3E1. 604-685-4160; fax: 604-689-4118.

Noreen Ayres. c/o Sourcebooks, Inc., Unstoppable, P.O. Box 372, Naperville, IL 60566, e-mail: Noreenayr@AOL.com.

Officer Wayne Barton. Barton's Boosters, 1515 North Federal Highway, Suite 222, Boca Raton, FL 33432, 561-391-2942.

Tim Bearer. c/o Sourcebooks, Inc., Unstoppable, P.O. Box 372, Naperville, IL 60566.

Gertrude Boyle. Columbia Sportswear, 6600 N. Baltimore, Portland, Oregon 97203.

Linda Bremner. Love Letters, Inc., 436 A Eisenhower Lane, Lombard, IL 60148. 630-620-1970.

Dr. Francisco Bucio. c/o Sourcebooks, Inc., Unstoppable, P.O. Box 372, Naperville, IL 60566.

Stephen Cannell. c/o Sourcebooks, Inc., Unstoppable, P.O. Box 372, Naperville, IL 60566.

George Dantzig. c/o Sourcebooks, Inc., Unstoppable, P.O. Box 372, Naperville, IL 60566.

Lee Dunham. McDonald's Corporation, 41 Grand Avenue, Suite 103, River Edge, NJ 07661.

Maxcy D. Filer. Law Office, 363 West Compton Blvd., Compton, CA 90220.

Millard & Linda Fuller. Habitat for Humanity International, 121 Habitat Street, Americus, GA 31709-3498, 800-HABITAT.

Evelynne Glennie. P.O. Box 6, Sawtry, Huntingdon, Cambridgeshire, PE17 5WE, United Kingdom 27. e-mail: eghq@evelyn.co.uk.

Olivia Goldsmith. c/o Harper Collins, 10 E. 53rd Street, NY, NY 10022.

Barbara Grogan. Western Industrial Contractors, 5301 Joliet Street, Denver, CO 80239.

Eula Hall. Mud Creek Clinic, P.O. Box 129, Grethel, KY 41631.

Tom Harken. Tom Harken & Associates, 8050 Eastex Freeway, Beaumont, TX 77708.

Dick & Rick Hoyt. RR #2 Box 1395, Holland, MA 01521, 413-245-9466.

Maria Elena Ibanez. International High Tech Marketing, 1441 NW 89th Court, Miami, FL 33172.

Craig Kielburger. Free the Children, 12 East 48th Street, New York, NY 10017. 905-881-0863. fax: 905-881-1849, e-mail: Freechild@CLO.com, www.freethechildren.org

Ken Kragen. c/o Sourcebooks, Inc., Unstoppable, P.O. Box 372, Naperville, IL 60566.

Pam Lontos. Lontos Sales & Motivation, Inc., P.O. Box 617553, Orlando, FL 32861-7553; 407-299-6128: fax: 407-299-2166.

John Mautner. The Nutty Bavarian, 791 First Street, Altamonte Springs, FL 32701. 407-767-0001, fax: 407-767-8811.

Tom Monaghan. Domino's Pizza, Inc., 30 Frank Lloyd Wright Drive, Ann Arbor, MI 48106-0997.

Laura-Beth Moore. c/o Sourcebooks, Inc., Unstoppable, P.O. Box 372, Naperville, IL 60566.

Shirley Muldowney. c/o Sourcebooks, Inc., Unstoppable, P.O. Box 372, Naperville, IL 60566.

Diana Nyad. c/o Sourcebooks, Inc., Unstoppable, P.O. Box 372, Naperville, IL 60566.

Paul Orfalea. Kinko's, Inc., P.O. Box 8000, Ventura, CA 93002-8000.

Billy Payne. NationsBank, 600 Peachtree Street NE, 55th Floor, Atlanta, GA 30308-2214.

Sheri Poe. P.O. Box 215, Newton Center, MA 02159.

Bill Porter. To contact Bill Porter to order Watkins products, call 1-800-WATKINS and reference his account #66761. Bill and his long-time friend and associate, Shelly Brady, are available for motivational keynote presentations and can be reached at 3100 Northeast 33rd, Portland, OR 97212. 503-760-9341.

Sharlyne R. Powell. Women at Large/Ladyfit Fitness Club, 1020 South 48th Avenue, Yakima, WA 98908.

Joan Rivers. c/o Sourcebooks, Inc., Unstoppable, P.O. Box 372, Naperville, IL 60566.

Rocky Robinson. Bedford-Stuyvesant Volunteer Ambulance Corps, 213 Marcus Garvey Blvd., Brooklyn, NY 11221. 718-453-4617.

Ms. Suzan Robison. c/o Sourcebooks, Inc., Unstoppable, P.O. Box 372, Naperville, IL 60566.

Anita Roddick. The Body Shop International, Watersmead, Little Hampton, West Suffex, BN 176LS, England.

The Honorable Leah J. Sears. Supreme Court of Georgia, 501 State Judicial Building, Atlanta, GA 30334.

Carolyn Stradley. C&S Paving, P.O. Box 1155, Marietta, GA 30061.

Jackie Torrence. 2143 Statesville Blvd., Box 264-C, Salisbury, NC 28147.

Mary Joan Willard. NTI, Helping Hands, 1505 Commonwealth Avenue Boston, MA 02135. 617-787-4419.

Maury Wills. 837 Sandhill Avenue, Carson, CA 90746.

Kemmons Wilson. Kemmons Wilson Companies, 1629 Winchester Road, Memphis, TN 38116-3504.

Index

index

index